Flying
CARS

THE TRUE STORY

BY
ANDREW GLASS

Clarion Books

HOUGHTON MIFFLIN HARCOURT

Boston • New York

Clarion Books
215 Park Avenue South
New York, New York 10003

Clarion Books is an imprint of Houghton Mifflin Harcourt Publishing Company.

www.hmhco.com

The text was set in Perpetua.
Book design by Trish Parcell Watts

Library of Congress Cataloging-in-Publication Data
Glass, Andrew, 1949–, author.
Flying cars / by Andrew Glass.
pages cm
Includes bibliographical references and index.
Summary: Flying cars are real! This book for young readers combines history, biography, technology, and humor
in a breezy survey of hybrid vehicles and the dream of flight that kept inventors at work despite many failures and
the dictates of common sense.—Provided by publisher.
Audience: Ages 9–12.
ISBN 978-0-618-98482-4 (hardcover) —
1. Flying automobiles—History—Juvenile literature. 2. Flying automobiles—Technological innovations—
Juvenile literature. 3. Inventors—Biography—Juvenile literature. I. Title.
TL684.8.G53 2015
629.04—dc23
2014027740

Manufactured in China
SCP 10 9 8 7 6 5 4 3 2 1
4500528913

For Joann and Katherine

The desire to fly is an idea handed down by our ancestors who, in their grueling travels across the trackless lands in prehistoric times, looked enviously on the birds soaring freely through space, at full speed, above all obstacles, on the infinite highway of the air.

—Wilbur Wright

"Maybe you should try thinking about the future for a change."

". . . You mean, what, like flying cars?"

—Michael Chabon, *The Yiddish Policemen's Union*

CONTENTS

1

FIRST, THE DREAM

Cars fly every day—in fantasy. They soar by pure magic, like the Weasley family car in the Harry Potter series, or by sprouting wings, like Chitty Chitty Bang Bang. Some use high-tech gadgetry, allowing well-equipped heroes like James Bond and Batman to make incredible cliffhanger escapes.

But visionary engineers and inventors haven't just imagined flying cars. Some actually built them . . . and then drove them up into the sky.

On the night of September 4, 1882, inventor Thomas Edison (1847–1931) turned on the lights. His generator on Pearl Street produced enough electricity to light up four hundred light bulbs in eighty homes in New York City, thus ushering in an era of modern techno-magic. The early years of the twentieth century witnessed a multitude of astonishing technological advances: wireless radio communication . . . recorded sound and moving pictures . . . horseless carriages that were powered instead by steam, electricity, or gasoline . . . and, most remarkable of all, flying machines. When the first daring birdmen took to the air aboard their heavier-than-air flying machines, they accomplished what nearly everyone—including scientists—had deemed to be impossible, a fantasy.

Ancient-world storytellers told the tale of an inventor named Daedalus,

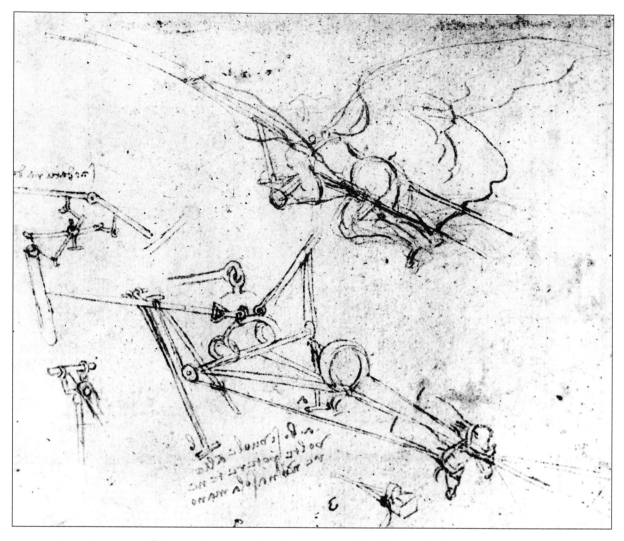

A muscle-powered flying machine, based on the structure of birds' wings, by Leonardo da Vinci, 1490.
The aviator would lie facedown and work the wings with his arms and legs.

who constructed wings out of feathers and wax for himself and his son, Icarus. They strapped the homemade wings to their backs and leaped from a cliff. Young Icarus foolishly soared too close to the sun. The wax melted, and the boy plummeted into the sea. Daedalus flapped sadly off to freedom, proving that his artificial wing design was entirely functional, at least mythologically speaking.

Inventor Leonardo da Vinci (1452–1519) studied birds in flight. He made many analytical drawings of their wings and then designed a human-powered flying machine. He also came up with the idea for a car propelled by a tightly wound spring. Although Leonardo lacked an actual engine to power his devices, his designs were not mythological tall tales; they were real plans—concepts that anticipated transportation technologies hundreds of years in the future.

Midway through the nineteenth century, a French sea captain, Jean Marie Le Bris (1817–1872), was inspired by the flight of the albatross, a large seabird. Like da Vinci, he made meticulous studies of how the bird's aerodynamic shape aids its movement through the air. Then, using his knowledge of ship design, Le Bris stretched cloth over wood and constructed a glider with a 50-foot wingspan. He designed pedals to raise and lower the glider's tail, and hand levers to adjust the angle of the wings. He wanted to simulate the subtle interaction between wings and air that controlled the direction of the albatross's flight and gave the bird its ability to stay aloft so effortlessly. He also built a

Patent drawing for the Albatross.

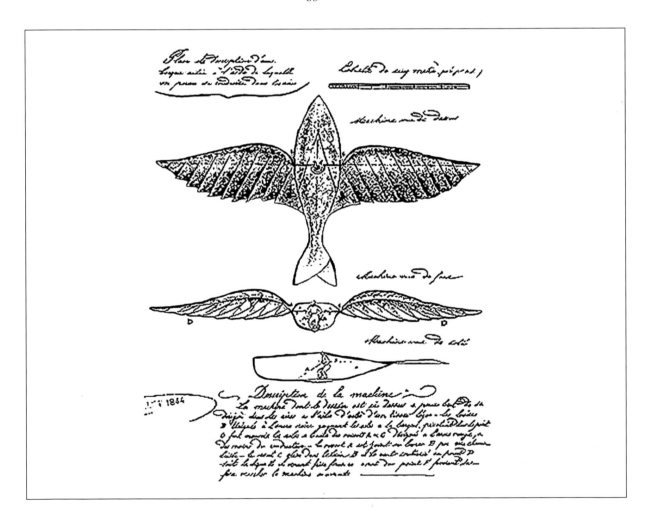

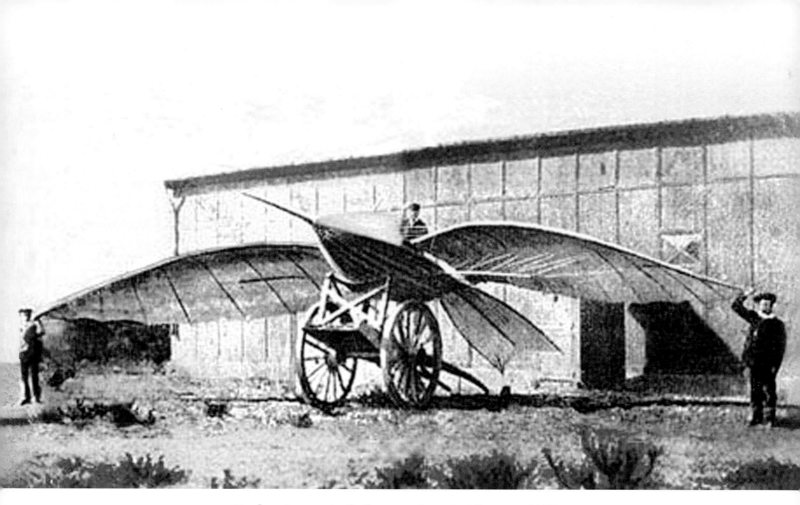

The first photograph of a flying machine: the Albatross, *1868.*

horse-drawn cart for carrying and launching his mechanical bird, and in 1857 he applied for a patent for an artificial albatross or aerial car.

Eyewitness accounts of the aerial car's trial run described how Le Bris instructed his driver to race the cart along a road while heading directly into the wind. Atop the cart was the *Albatross,* courageously piloted by Captain Le Bris himself. It caught a 10-knot breeze and soared majestically some 300 feet into the air—along with the unfortunate cart driver, who'd become snagged in a restraining rope and was dangling behind. The glider itself and the unlucky driver sustained only minor damage on landing.

Le Bris rebuilt the *Albatross,* but further attempts to launch it ended badly. Finally the aerial car was demolished during a disastrous landing that also broke the inventor's leg. This concluded Le Bris's wheels-to-wings adventure. However, his aerial car was the first aircraft to be piloted to a higher altitude than its point of departure, and also the first flying machine to be photographed.

2

$\mathcal{G}$USTAVE WHITEHEAD'S *CONDOR*

When he was a boy, Gustav Albin Weiss-kopf (1874–1927) fabricated a pair of wings and leaped from the roof of his grandparents' house in Ansbach, Germany. He wanted to see if he would fly. He didn't. At the age of thirteen, he was apprenticed to a machinist and learned how to build engines. He left Germany in the late 1880s, and eventually he arrived in America an experienced sailor and machinist. He was hired by a Harvard professor as the chief mechanic in charge of testing experimental kites, and he also constructed gliders for the Boston Aeronautical Society, following well-established designs. By 1897, he'd successfully made short flights. In New York

City he built and flew kites engineered to carry a man's weight. Scientific kite flying, as it was called, was cutting-edge aviation technology at the time.

This lithograph of a Whitehead airship (glider) appeared in the New York Herald *on October 4, 1897.*

In Buffalo, New York, he changed his name to Gustave Whitehead so he would sound more American. He called himself Gus and began referring to himself as an aeronaut. From Buffalo he moved to Pittsburgh and then on to Baltimore, taking employment as a factory worker, a coal miner, and a skilled repairman. He moved to Bridgeport, Connecticut, where he found work as a night watchman. In each city he resolutely continued his research into manned flight, and he constructed and publicly demonstrated his airships. He was certain that the right motor would make powered flight possible, so he worked to perfect his engines, making them smaller and lighter. In Pittsburgh he created a glider equipped with a steam engine of his own design. A friend and collaborator later swore that they flew a steam-powered airship into a brick building, resulting in a fiery crash—which was followed by a vigorous request from the Pittsburgh police that they cease their dubious experiments or leave town. According to Whitehead, the flight was "more or less successful."

Convinced that some form of privately owned flying vehicle would one day become a part of daily life, Whitehead began formulating plans to build a passenger airship that could be adapted for

Gus Whitehead holding the Condor's *10-horsepower ground engine, 1901.*

driving along the road to a public park, field, or open meadow for taking off. He believed that airships needed to be drivable, like the motorized carriages of his day, and also function in the water if they were to efficiently transport aeronauts like himself to their destinations.

In a shed behind his house on Pine Street in Bridgeport, Whitehead re-engineered a conventional bird-shaped glider that he'd built in New York. He called it the *Condor 21,* after the large birds he'd watched soaring effortlessly off the coast of South America. With its boat-shaped gondola, where the pilot could sit or stand while operating the control stick, his airship resembled the *Albatross* glider of Captain Le Bris, another experienced sailor. But the two-passenger vehicle didn't need a horse for locomotion. Whitehead had designed and built two engines powered by a series of rapid gas explosions. The smaller engine produced enough piston pressure to provide 10 horsepower to the front wheels for driving. The larger 20-horsepower engine added more power for taking off and to spin two propellers, which were designed to counter-rotate for stability in the air. The *Condor*'s 36-foot wings, made of bamboo poles covered with canvas, could be folded into nine segments

A different view of the Condor *with Whitehead, his assistants, and his daughter, Rose, 1901.*

and stored against the cabin. A flat fan-shaped tail controlled the ascent and descent of the *Condor* in flight.

Just after midnight on August 14, 1901, Gustave Whitehead, with an assistant aboard, slowly drove his 16-foot-long flying automobile, its wings neatly folded, along Pine Street in Bridgeport. The entire contraption rode on four small wooden wheels. Reaching a paved stretch of road, they raced off at an estimated 20 to 30 miles per hour. A second assistant and a reporter from the *Bridgeport Herald* kept up as best they could on bicycles. Later, in the first light of dawn, both engines were tested and every structural joint and rod examined. By early morning they had succeeded in making an unmanned trial flight. According to one account, a milkman who'd stopped in the road nearly lost control of his startled horse when the *Condor*'s outstretched wings flapped in the breeze.

Whitehead took his place in the gondola and opened the throttle of the ground engine. The vehicle motored along for a hundred yards, picking up speed, and then he flipped the lever, adding the ground engine's power to that of the more powerful propeller engine. The same lever caused the wing canvas to spring taut. Instantly, the bow lifted and the airship shot up in the air like a kite, powered by its twin propellers. The *Condor* reportedly chugged along in a straight line fifty feet above the ground until Whitehead realized that he was not going to clear the stand of chestnut trees that lay ahead. He may have tried altering the speed of the individual propellers to control the airship in flight, or maybe he tried to bend the wings with the control stick, which was attached to guide wires. In any event, dramatically shifting his weight to one side at the last moment caused the *Condor* to veer from its course, banking around the danger. After motoring through the air for more than a mile, he shut down the engines and landed the *Condor* lightly on its four wooden wheels. "That was the happiest moment of my life, for I had demonstrated that the machine I have worked on for so many years would do what I claimed for it. It was a grand sensation to be flying through the air. There is nothing like it."

The August 18, 1901, edition of the *Bridgeport Herald* carried a full-page article stating that Gus Whitehead's *Condor* had flown near Bridgeport, Connecticut. Newspapers all over America and around the world picked up the story of his achievement in a "flying automobile."

Another *Condor*—with a foldable tail, rear-wheel steering, improved engines, and silk-covered wings over ribs made

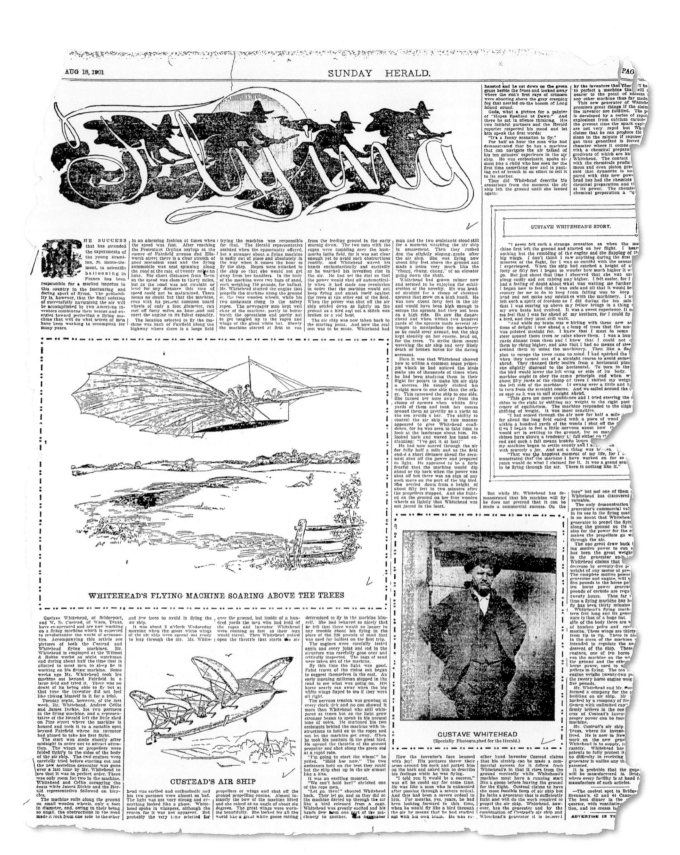

The Bridgeport Herald *reports Whitehead's success, August 18, 1901.*

of steel and aluminum tubing—was reported to have made even longer flights. But in spite of its notable success as a flying machine, it proved difficult to control in high winds. Whitehead abandoned experimenting with "roadable" airships to pursue the more reliable business of supplying his efficient, lightweight motors to other pioneering aviators.

Some flight historians have contested Whitehead's claim (and that of his supporters) that his flying automobile preceded the Wright brothers into the air by more than two years. They remain unconvinced that the *Condor* ever got off the ground. Others have acknowledged Whitehead's flight as history's first manned, powered, controlled, sustained flight in a heavier-than-air craft.

Despite controversy, the chronicle of Gustave Whitehead's flying automobile marks a possibility that arose in the early years of the twentieth century. Instead of branching into two completely separate machines, one for driving and one for flying, motorized travel might have evolved into a personal transportation machine with wings for flying and wheels for driving. However, the Wright brothers' *Flyer* (which didn't even have wheels for takeoff, let alone drivability) was designed with greater potential for controlled flight than the

Researchers in a German museum created a replica of the Condor. *It flew successfully in 1998, lending further support to Whitehead's claim that he successfully flew such an aircraft in 1901.*

Condor and proved more suitable for both commercial and military purposes. So instead of being embraced from the start, the flying car became something like a recurring dream, a technological ideal to be pursued and promoted by a few determined inventors in the new century.

On June 26, 2013, Connecticut governor Dannel P. Malloy signed into law a measure declaring that Gustave Whitehead of Bridgeport, Connecticut, flew a flying automobile in 1901, more than two years before Orville Wright claimed to have successfully motored from atop a sand dune at Kitty Hawk, North Carolina.

3

TRAJAN VUIA'S *AÉROPLANE-AUTOMOBILE*

In 1903, Trajan (also spelled Traian) Vuia (1872–1950), a young Romanian lawyer from a small village in Transylvania, submitted a proposal to the Science Academy of Paris announcing his intention to construct an airplane-automobile.

The Science Academy's Special Commission on Aeronautics called Vuia's proposal (*"Projet d'Aéroplane-automobile"*) unrealistic. "The problem of flight with a machine weighing more than air cannot be solved," the commission stated.

This drawing of a propeller-driven car accompanied Vuia's patent application for his aéroplane-automobile in 1903.

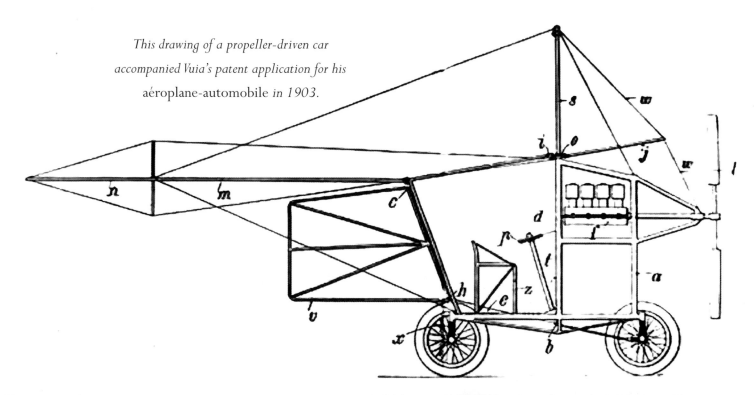

"It is only a dream." In October, seemingly unaffected by the reports of Whitehead's success, an article in the *New York Times* declared, "The flying machine which will really fly might be evolved by the combined and continuous efforts of mathematicians and mechanicians in from one million to 10 million years."

Over the winter of 1902, Vuia had constructed a simple automobile of tubular steel with a front-mounted propeller. Despite the prevailing view—based on glider experiments—that any flying machine required at least a double-wing (biplane) design, the *Vuia 1* had only a single wing. It measured 8.70 meters (28.5 feet). In defense of his design (that is, of one wing on each side), Vuia said simply, "I have never seen a bird with more than two wings."

By December 1905, Vuia had begun testing his automobile by careening around an isolated plain called Montesson, near Paris. Adding the wings trans-

Vuia's drivable wingless automobile.

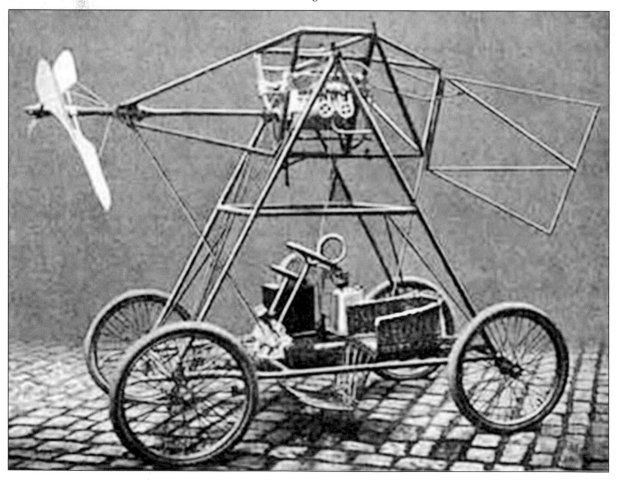

But Vuia, unhurt, considered it a triumph. It wasn't a long flight, nor had the vehicle attained an impressive altitude, but Vuia was publicly acknowledged to have succeeded in driving, taking off, flying, and landing again in a fully functional airplane-automobile. No one doubted that the machine had accomplished what its inventor had set out to do. It was no fantasy—it was reality. A *New York Herald* headline announced, "Vuia Airplane Makes a Successful Flight."

ABOVE: *Airborne!*

Vuia's trial run has been widely acknowledged as the first unaided takeoff in aviation history
and the first flight of an airplane-automobile.

BELOW: *A hard landing.*

Vuia preparing for a trial takeoff and landing.

formed the vehicle into what he called his airplane-automobile. He hoped his kerosene-powered 20-horsepower engine would create enough propulsion for takeoff without any of the external assistance needed for previous flights, such as the wheeled cart of Captain Le Bris or the sloping wooden track used by the Wright brothers. Successful independent takeoff and landing would prove that a hybrid personal transportation machine operated by a lone pilot/driver was not only possible but feasible. But Vuia remained earthbound until he felt confident driv-

ing at 40 kilometers per hour (25 miles per hour).

Finally, on March 19, 1906, at three o'clock in the afternoon, before an audience of local gentry, fellow inventors, and journalists, Vuia drove his airplane-automobile about 50 meters (164 feet), ascended into the air to a height of about 1 meter (3.28 feet), and powered ahead for 12 meters (39.5 feet) before the engine fizzled, which caused the propeller to stop turning. The *aéroplane-automobile* tilted to the left and landed hard, damaging the left front wheel.

An announcement of Trajan Vuia's success appeared in the New York Herald. *A lithographer "repaired" the damaged wheel for the engraving.*

But was the vehicle an airplane, as the *New York Herald* headline suggested, or a flying car, as its name suggested? Though it looked like a horseless carriage with wings, its wheeled frame could also be considered the revolutionary undercarriage for a primitive airplane. *L'Aèrophile,* the official journal of L'Aero-Club de France, seems to have agreed with the *Herald.* After witnessing a preliminary trial, a columnist declared that Mr. Vuia was the first person in France to have attempted, with a machine able to carry a man, the direct takeoff of an airplane.

The *aéroplane-automobile*'s propeller might have given people the idea that it was indeed meant to be an airplane, since a car driven by whirling propeller blades would, at the very least, create a havoc of flying hats and umbrellas, litter, and dust along the boulevard, and likely put pedestrians at serious risk. However, in spite of the obvious disadvantages and safety hazards, there weren't any legal restrictions against a propeller-driven car. (Vuia's airplane-automobile wasn't the only one of its kind. In 1922, Marcel Leyat, a French aircraft builder, attempted to market the Helica. Though derived from the new airplane technology, the Helica was designed as a propeller-driven automobile, not a flying machine.)

The *aéroplane-automobile*'s four rubber tires weren't standard equipment on experimental flying machines in those days, and neither were the folding wings on the redesigned *Vuia 2*. Both innovations suggest that the inventor intended to build a new type of transportation machine, one that would function as a practical flying machine and also as an automobile. One published authority puts the *Vuia 1* squarely in the flying car category, at the top of his chronology: "1906 Trajan Vuia tests flying auto near Paris, France." Another aircraft historian reports having gathered substantive proof, including the inventor's notes to that effect, that Vuia's airplane-automobile was unequivocally meant as a flying car.

In 1906, flying machines and driving machines were not yet understood to be separate transportation technologies. But the difficulty of actually constructing a flying/driving vehicle led most pioneering aeronautical engineers to abandon the idea of a unified machine and to pursue the airplane as a separate mechanical entity with its own aerodynamic requirements. Rugged horseless carriages were left to evolve into bulky, comfortable passenger cars without wings.

Marcel Leyat claimed to have received six hundred orders for his propeller-driven Helica.

Vuia with his folding-wing aéroplane-automobile, *which looks as if it was designed to be both driven and flown.*

Vuia flew his folding-wing airplane-automobile successfully throughout 1907. Though he never flew farther than 24 meters (79 feet), he felt confident in declaring that the problem of flight had been solved. What remained was to industrialize aviation—an important mission, he admitted, but not to be confused with creation of the new machine.

Following the crash of a folding-wing prototype, Vuia moved on to experimental helicopters, but not before Wilbur Wright had witnessed a demonstration of the airplane-automobile during a visit he made to France in 1908. Soon after, the Wright brothers abandoned their track-assisted takeoff in favor of wheels for taking off and landing.

4

GLENN CURTISS'S AUTOPLANE

With few exceptions, anyone driving beyond the city limits anywhere in the United States at the turn of the twentieth century could expect to encounter not paved roads but muddy horse trails full of bone-jarring ruts. Faced with such harsh driving conditions, pioneer motorists must have longed for some sort of airplane-automobile. Glenn Hammond Curtiss (1878–1930) actually built one.

Curtiss was born in Hammondsport, New York. His family moved to New York City, where he completed the eighth grade. He worked as a Western Union bike messenger and then opened his own bicycle shop. He converted a bicycle to a one-cylinder motorcycle (with a carbu-

retor made from a tomato can) and went into the motorcycle business. In 1907, astride a spindly motorcycle of his own design with a 40-horsepower V8 engine

Glenn Curtiss's motorcycle feat earned him the title "Fastest Man on Earth."

June Bug *won the Scientific American Trophy, the first aeronautical prize to be awarded in the United States.*

and no brakes, he traveled at the record-breaking, extremely precarious speed of 136 miles per hour.

Curtiss's success in building superior lightweight motors brought him to the attention of Alexander Graham Bell, renowned inventor of the telephone. Bell, together with his wife, Mabel Gardiner Hubbard, was pursuing other avenues of scientific inquiry, including flight. Convinced that a heavier-than-air vehicle could be designed to fly, Hubbard provided the inspiration and financing to establish the Aerial Experiment Association, with a mandate to construct "a practical flying aerodrome or flying ma-

chine driven through the air by its own power and carrying a man."

Curtiss became Director of Experiments at the Aerial Experiment Association. On July 4, 1908, their prototype airplane, *June Bug,* took the Scientific American Trophy in the distance competition by flying nearly a mile. On May 29, 1910, after nearly two years of developing his prototype, Curtiss completed a 150-mile flight along the Hudson River from Albany, New York, to Manhattan. This was by far the longest flight yet attempted in the United States, ushering in the age of modern air travel. Hailed as a phenomenal technological accomplishment,

The first-ever official pilot's license, issued to
Glen Curtiss by the Aero Club of America
on June 8, 1911.

Curtiss's unprecedented achievement received six full pages of text and photos in the *New York Times*—the most space the newspaper had ever allotted to a single news event.

That same year, Curtiss moved his operation to San Diego and founded the Curtiss Aeroplane Company. In 1911, he was issued the first pilot's license, Aviator's License number one, by the Aero Club of America. His company, which was renamed the Curtiss Aeroplane and Motor Company in 1916, built a plane for the navy that could take off from a ship. The Curtiss *Triad* was the first "hydroaeroplane." It was a multiuse airplane capable of taking off from and landing in the water as well as on solid ground.

After Curtiss successfully landed the *Triad* on North Island near San Diego, a boy named Waldo overheard him saying, "Now if we could just take the wings off and drive this down the road, we'd really have something!" Waldo took the remark to heart. Meanwhile, Curtiss got his team busy designing a flying car.

Predictors of early twentieth-century technology had already imagined that just as the horse-drawn carriage was already being replaced on the road by the horseless carriage, earthbound automobiles would soon be replaced by flying machines designed for personal transportation. Horseless carriages (automobiles), like those introduced to the United States in 1896, were not very different from pioneering aircraft. Both were made possible by the invention of an efficient internal combustion engine: an explosion (fuel ignited by

Early promotion for the Autoplane.

a spark) pushed a piston in a cylinder, which turned a driveshaft connected to a rear axle, which turned the wheels of the automobile, or turned a crankshaft that rotated the airplane's propeller. To function as practical personal transportation, both the automobile and the airplane required a fuel tank, some sort of steering device, a passenger cabin, a baggage compartment, at least three wheels, a battery, an engine, and a way to direct power from the engine to the propeller or wheels.

In addition, an airplane needed wings, a rudder, ailerons, a propeller, a horizontal stabilizer, and a vertical tail, none of which are required by an automobile. An automobile, on the other hand, needed a durable suspension system to absorb the shocks and jolts resulting from driving on an irregular road surface and to help the car maintain contact with the road, and bumpers with enough strength and resistance to deal with ordinary bumps and bangs. It could also include such conveniences as mirrors, movable windows, and glove boxes. So from the beginning, the challenge facing a would-be flying car inventor was to build an automobile durable and stable enough to withstand the ruts, bumps, and uncertainties of driving, yet also light and aerodynamic enough to fly smoothly through the air.

And from the beginning, critics insisted that engineering compromises necessary to meet that challenge would make a truly practical flying car a technological impossibility.

Flying in the face of such down-to-earth engineering wisdom, Glenn Curtiss introduced the Curtiss Autoplane at the 1917 Pan-American Aeronautic Exposition in New York City. The 27-foot-long all-aluminum triple-winged airplane could be disassembled and driven down the street. Later, the chauffeur/pilot could attach the one-piece tail

RIGHT: *The Autoplane's windshield and windows were made of celluloid, an early form of plastic.*

BELOW: *This photo of the Autoplane without its flight component was taken on June 5, 1917. It appeared in a brochure for the 1917 Pan-American Aeronautic Exposition.*

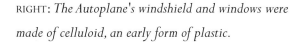

and the 40-foot wing section, and switch the chain-and-gear mechanism from the wheels to the four-blade wooden pusher propeller, mounted behind the cabin. Then the Autoplane would take off and soar through the clouds (and over the ruts and the muck) at a steady 65 miles per hour while two passengers relaxed in the comfort of its posh leather-lined, velvet-curtained compartment.

In 1921, a French inventor, René Tampier, built a spindly in-line two-seater vehicle with hinged wings that folded along its sides. *L'Avion-Automobile* (airplane-motorcar) was a fully functioning flying machine, designed so that when the

This photograph of the Curtiss Autoplane with wings attached
was retouched for the cover of the 1917 exposition brochure.

After a short flight to the seventh annual Salon de l'aviation *(aviation conference) in Paris,
the* Avion-Automobile *drove around the city backwards for two hours, reaching a speed of 15 miles per hour.*

French countryside was enshrouded in fog, the craft could be landed safely and then driven to its destination. It was powered by a second motor attached to its removable back wheels. A prototype was photographed lumbering tail-first down a Parisian boulevard at 15 miles per hour.

L'Avion-Automobile functioned as a "road-able" airplane, meaning it was primarily an airplane but was also practical and legal to drive, though not necessarily intended for extensive use on the street, like a car. The Curtiss Autoplane (also called the Flying Limousine), once disengaged from its removable fuselage, wings, and tail component, transported its high-toned passengers down the street in what was unquestionably a chauffeured motorcar, not an awkward folding airplane on temporary wheels. This made it the first unambiguous flying car, even though it may never have actually flown well or very far . . . or possibly even at all. And though admittedly an odd-looking automobile, it would not have been the only peculiar vehicle on the road in 1917.

World War I (1914–18) greatly increased the demand for military aircraft, and the Curtiss Aeroplane and Motor Company's enthusiasm for its flying limo was replaced by the more pressing quest to build a military training plane that was both easy to fly and easy to maintain.

The result was the JN-4, nicknamed the Jenny. It was the first mass-produced American airplane, and thousands of military pilots and pioneering birdmen (and -women, too) learned to fly in one. After the war, surplus Curtiss Jennys became the plane of choice for daredevil stunt pilots, who were called barnstormers because of their tendency to fly low over farm buildings as a way of advertising their flying shows. Barnstormers flew around the country, performing aerial acrobatics and selling rides, often in a used Jenny bought at auction. During the 1920s, plenty of eager Americans took their first airplane ride with a barnstormer in a simple, reliable Curtiss Jenny.

The one and only Autoplane prototype was dismantled and its parts used to build an experimental flying boat for the military. In 1921, Glenn Curtiss merged his company with its former competitor, Wright Aeronautical, forming the Curtiss-Wright Company. He became a successful real estate developer in Florida and died in 1930 following appendix surgery.

This advertising poster for a flying circus depicts barnstormers performing an aerial feat in Curtiss Jennys.

5

FELIX LONGOBARDI'S COMBINATION VEHICLE

The aluminum Curtiss Autoplane is widely credited with being the first flying car, but the first U.S. government patent for a flying car was awarded to Felix Longobardi, on December 3, 1918.

Longobardi proposed a "combination vehicle" that could be driven overland on four wheels, powered through water by propellers, and flown through the air while held aloft by retractable wings and powered by the same dual propellers in the stern (rear) that pushed it forward through water. Longobardi's dream vehicle also came fully equipped with the latest in radio antennas and four cannons. Not surprisingly, this remarkable vehicle never existed, except on paper.

Seventy-six official U.S. patent applications for flying cars have been chronicled, beginning with Longobardi's. However, a leading expert claims to have found nearly 1,800 patents for flying cars and roadable aircraft, and has identified more than 2,300 such projects overall. Three hundred may have actually flown. No one knows how many drawings, fanciful models, and unworkable prototypes were hammered together in backyards by tinkerers who never applied for a patent. In the words of one aviation historian, "There are dozens of roadables that never left the paper stage and remain drawings of dreams of the designers who were unable to build them."

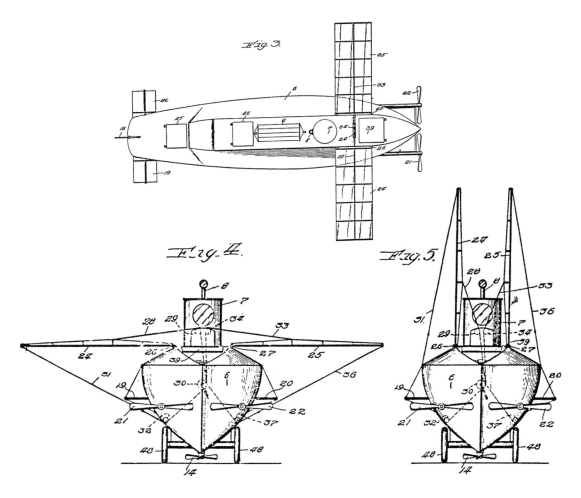

Fig. 3.

Fig. 4.

Fig. 5.

Drawings of Felix Longobardi's combination vehicle showing wheels, wings, underside propellers, and cannons.

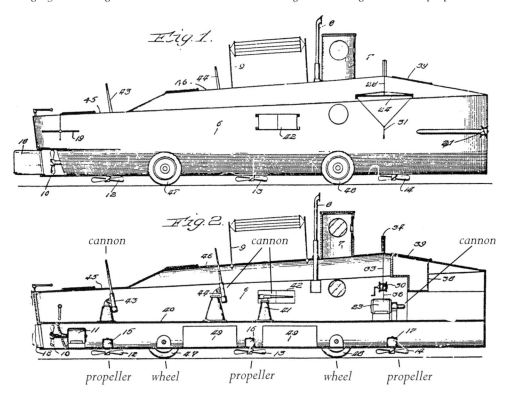

Fig. 1.

Fig. 2.

cannon   cannon   cannon

propeller   wheel   propeller   wheel   propeller

6

HENRY FORD'S FLYING FLIVVER

Henry Ford (1863–1947) is famous for his idea of having each factory worker perform a single repetitive task. Organizing work in this manner made mass production possible and efficient. It was Ford's intention to turn out a 20-horsepower five-passenger automobile that would suit the wallet of the assembly line worker who built it. The first Model T Ford automobile rattled off the assembly line on October 1, 1908. But at $850, while less than a third of the price of other automobiles, it was still beyond the reach of the well-paid Ford workers, who made five dollars a day. Most factory workers earned half that much. Nonetheless, the mass-produced Ford Model T (nicknamed the Tin Lizzie) set in motion the idea that any go-getter might aspire to own and drive a shiny symbol of the new twentieth-century American dream of independence: the freedom of the open road.

Unfortunately for even the fortunate few who could afford an automobile, there weren't many open roads or road signs back then, and road maps didn't become available until 1924. Mules still had the right of way, refueling stations were oddities, and cantankerous farmers complained that the cacophonous backfiring of jalopies caused distemper in their cows.

But further improvements in assembly-line production brought the price of a new Ford down to less than $300, and the motoring public's ever-growing passion for affordable, mass-produced cars led to a profusion of road-building projects. By the 1920s, new smoothly paved highways allowed automobiles to evolve from rugged horseless carriages such as Ford's Model T—which could even be used to power farm machinery when not bumping along the muddy country roads for which it was built—to comfortable, even luxurious family transportation sporting newfangled comforts such as automatic starters, motor-driven windshield wipers, headlights, and roll-down windows. An automobile—generally a Ford of some sort and popularly called a flivver, presumably a reference to the sound of the engine—was finally within the purchasing power of factory workers and farmers. Upwards of 30,000 flivvers soon clogged the newly paved roadways.

Pioneering aviators were just as passionate about their airplanes as early motorists were about their automobiles. They firmly believed that if airplanes could be made easier and safer to fly, drivers would take to the sky in automobile-sized airplanes. Charles Lindbergh became an international sensation in 1927 as the first birdman to fly an airplane alone across the Atlantic. Lindbergh's phenomenal celebrity inspired an enthusiastic rush to manufacture just such an easy-to-fly airplane. But even

Typical road, 1920.

Ford introduced its flying flivver with a publicity photo of Will Rogers,
comedian and commentator. Rogers never actually flew the plane.

before that, back in 1925, Henry Ford ordered his engineers to build a prototype for an affordable little airplane. How little? they asked. "Small enough to fit inside my office," Ford answered.

In 1926, the Ford Motor Company introduced the Sky Flivver, a single-seat airplane. Weighing just 350 pounds and measuring a mere 22 feet across, it was called a pocket airplane because of its small size. Ford intended to mass-produce a plane that could be sold for the price of a Model T.

On February 21, 1928, Harry Brooks crashed
into the ocean off Melbourne, Florida.

But only four Sky Flivvers were built. Ford sadly shut down production after his friend Harry Brooks, a pilot, died while doing a promotional tour in one of the prototypes. Ford remained certain, however, that his flying flivver was an important step toward a flying car for the average Joe. "Mark my words," he said, "a combination airplane and motorcar is coming. You may smile, but it will come."

7

WALDO WATERMAN'S ARROWBILE

In 1930, working in the corner of an abandoned aircraft company hangar in Los Angeles, an aeronautical engineer named Waldo Waterman (1894–1976) built America's first tailless monoplane, called a flying wing. This was the same Waldo who, back in 1911, overheard Glenn Curtiss say, "Now if we could just take the wings off and drive this down the road, we'd really have something!" Waldo's low-wing airplane taxied on three wheels, a steerable nose wheel in front and two wheels in back. Its pusher propeller was positioned where one expected the tail to be. It was so peculiar-looking that people often asked, "What is it?" Thus it became known around the Los Angeles airport as "Waterman's Whatsit." Unfortunately, the otherwise ingenious Whatsit proved too unbalanced for any but the most skilled pilot to operate.

In 1933, Eugene L. Vidal, director of the Bureau of Air Commerce under President Franklin D. Roosevelt, announced the Vidal Safety Airplane Competition (1933–36) to design and build a small plane that would be as comfortable and easy to operate as a car. Waterman believed that with just a little tweaking, his Whatsit would qualify. He redesigned and converted his swept-wing (low-wing) prototype to one with overhead wings for improved balance and

Waterman's Whatsit.

an unobstructed, therefore safer, view. He improved the maneuverability of the tricycle landing gear and simplified the interior, and in May 1935 he presented the rehabilitated Whatsit to the Bureau of Air Commerce with a new name, the Waterman Arrowplane.

The Arrowplane, which was the only proposal submitted by a solo inventor among the thirty "easy airplane" entries, received the first prize to be awarded. It was acknowledged to be a paragon of stability and simplicity for the novice pilot because it was nearly impossible to stall. A plane stalls when it loses lift by flying too slowly or by pulling incorrectly out of a dive or a turn. For an inexperienced pilot, stalling may lead to a dangerous downward corkscrew called a spin.

Waterman's Arrowplane was completely successful in all but one of the contest's primary criteria: it did not have

a selling price lower than $700. Indeed, with a price tag approaching $3,000, the Arrowplane wasn't even close. But none of the other entries—including the second award winner, Stearman-Hammond Company's corrugated metal Y-1 Machine, described by one critic as looking like "a flying tool shed"—met the affordability stipulation either.

Even though the Arrowplane was beyond the reach of the contest's hypothetical "everypilot," its acclaimed engineering success allowed Waterman to pursue his true dream: an airplane that could be driven down the street. Then (just as Curtiss before him had said) he'd really have something! He formed the Waterman Airplane Corporation of Santa Monica, California, with the financial backing of Transcontinental and Western Air and the Studebaker Corporation. He got to work devising detachable wings and a transmission capable of transferring power from the propeller, for flying, to the wheels, for driving. By 1937, his unbalanced little Whatsit, which had been transformed to a stable, easy-to-fly Arrowplane, had been transformed again, this time into a futuristic three-wheel flying car called the Waterman Arrowbile.

The Arrowbile was powered by a Studebaker automobile engine and equipped with a standard automobile battery and starter. It had various automobile incidentals, such as knobs from the Studebaker dashboard. It also sported an airspeed indicator, an altimeter (which displayed the altitude while

The Waterman Arrowbile drives out from under its resdesigned flight component. The original design required each wing to be removed separately.

flying), and an expensive magnetic compass, all on the dashboard. Waterman economized by using readily available Willys Jeep headlights, a small car steering wheel, and a Ford radiator grille. The only flight control was a wheel yoke (a double handle, somewhat like a steering wheel in form, suspended from the cabin ceiling in front of the pilot). This controlled the rudder and the ailerons. Moving the wheel yoke forward or back made the plane go up or down; turning the wheel yoke made the plane turn left or right, like a car. For driving, a gas pedal, foot brake, and parking brake were located on the floorboard. Once its quick-release detachable wings were removed, the Arrowbile cruised smoothly at up to 70 miles per hour on the road, looking like a nifty wingless Whatsit.

The Arrowbile on the road.

Waldo prepares to go for a spin.

Because the Arrowbile had three wheels and one headlight, it was classified and licensed as a motorcycle. However, it was the first truly functional flying car.

Intended for the novice pilot, the Arrowbile proved every bit as reliable in flight as the award-winning Arrowplane. It flew at a nearly spin-proof 120 miles per hour and was almost impossible to stall. Three wheels, lighter and less expensive to build than four, were considered adequate for driving under ordinary conditions. Indeed, three-wheel cars were not unheard of; the Goliath was manufac-

tured and sold in Germany during the belt-tightening years of the 1930s, and several with characteristically playful names such as the Frisky, Family Three, and Scootacar have been produced since.

Unfortunately, the few drivers who could afford an expensive, fashionable ride during the Great Depression wanted the heavy chrome and rich leather of a luxury car, not a three-wheel wingless Whatsit, no matter how sleek it was. In addition, Waterman's Arrowbile was criticized for its poor road handling and its lightweight construction, which raised fears that even a minor road accident might render it unsafe to fly. Only five Arrowbiles were ever constructed. But what sidelined the Arrowbile was not its futuristic appearance or its possible engineering flaws. In 1938, Waterman's chief supporter, Harris M. Hanshue, the retired president of the airline that became TWA, died and, with him, the company's enthusiasm for the Arrowbile.

By this time, military preparation for yet another European war was putting a halt to civilian aircraft development. In addition, Waterman was incapacitated for nearly a year by a ruptured appendix. When he recovered his health, he developed one of the nation's largest civilian training programs to train aviators. He then became the chief engineer at Consolidated Vultee, an aircraft company. At Consolidated, later renamed Convair, he collaborated with other engineers, including his old friend Bill Stout, to create prototypes to meet the much-predicted postwar demand by returning pilots for small family-sized planes of their own. Waterman and his new colleagues became convinced that the most practical personal plane would be a flying car.

The first fully functional flying car, airborne!

8

HAROLD PITCAIRN'S AUTOGYRO

In 1919, Spanish inventor Juan de la Cierva (1895–1936) believed he'd invented an inherently safe aircraft. By 1923, he'd successfully demonstrated that his revolutionary machine could fly safely even at low speeds. Individually hinged overhead rotor blades generated lift, and the craft was propelled forward by a nose propeller like that on a conventional airplane. The unpowered overhead rotors were mounted on a mast and were set in motion by winding a rope around the mast and pulling it to start the rotors spinning. The rotors were kept spinning by the aircraft moving forward through the air. Stubby wings with ailerons also helped with lift and provided flight con-

trol in the air. De la Cierva named his invention the autogyro, which means "turns by itself." The Spanish trade name for it was Autogiro.

In 1929, de la Cierva went into business with Harold Pitcairn (1897–1960), an American aeronautical pioneer. Three years earlier, Pitcairn had designed a rugged airplane, the Mailwing, for the postal service. Pilots liked it because it was safe, easy to fly, fast, and reliable. De la Cierva and Pitcairn began their partnership by devising a way to make the Autogiro's rotors self-starting. They were able to accomplish this by directing the flow of air from the conventional front propeller toward the

Juan de la Cierva with his C-3 Autogiro, completed in June 1921.

tail flaps, which in turn redirected the air to the overhead rotors to start them spinning. Once the Autogiro was airborne, the same front propeller pulled the craft forward. Only a short runway was required for takeoff. Pitcairn boasted that their Autogiro could fly 100 miles per hour in all sorts of weather and land in a 30-foot area. He also claimed that it had the potential to be easily converted to a roadable vehicle with a powered tail wheel.

Although their self-starting Autogiro still looked like the sort of contraption Leonardo might have drawn back in

1490, Pitcairn and de la Cierva were awarded the 1930 Collier Trophy for the greatest achievement in aviation. One government official proclaimed, "Inventor Cierva and impresario Pitcairn offer the most promising flying machine in the thirty-year history of aviation."

President Herbert Hoover reserved for himself the honor of presenting the trophy so that he could get a gander at this revolutionary flying machine. A dramatic landing by the pilot James G. Ray on the White House lawn in 1931 made for exciting newsreel footage, creating an autogyro craze.

A Pitcairn Autogiro flying over New York City, fall 1930.

In 1931, James G. Ray landed an Autogiro on the South Lawn of the White House,
demonstrating its unique flying capabilities.

The celebrity pilot Amelia Earhart (1897–1937?), the first woman to cross the Atlantic in a plane, visited Pitcairn Aviation field in Willow Grove, Pennsylvania, and became the first woman to solo in an autogyro. When she set a new altitude record, the public's enthusiasm for the innovative aircraft soared. The response inspired Pitcairn to arrange for a spectacular promotional event: the first transcontinental autogyro flight. The event was sponsored by the Beech-Nut Chewing Gum Company, and the aircraft was piloted by the photogenic Earhart.

The publicity stunt would surely have been a notable triumph for Pitcairn's Autogiro, and might even have changed the course of aviation history, had it not been for Johnny Miller, a professional pilot. Miller, who had learned to fly at the Curtiss School of Flight in Mineola, New York, was the first person to place an order for an Autogiro. And as the first private Autogiro owner, he felt that he—not a glamorous celebrity pilot—should make the first coast-to-coast flight.

On May 14, 1931, after five short practice hops, Miller headed west in his brand-new Autogiro, which he had named *Missing Link.* Equipped with a compass and a road map, he used rivers and roads as landmarks. He made a side trip to the site of the Omaha Air

Amelia Earhart poses with the Beech-Nut Company's Autogiro.

Races, where he flew fourteen demonstration flights. *Missing Link* normally needed refueling every three hours, but strong headwinds made it burn so much fuel that Miller was forced to stop and install extra fuel tanks on the front seat. On May 28, he landed at North Island Naval Air Station in San Diego, California. The first transcontinental Autogiro trip had taken 43.8 hours in the air and was accomplished without mechanical incident.

With much fanfare, Earhart took off from Newark Airport on May 29 with a mechanic on board. She was in no particular hurry, making as many as ten publicity stops a day. When she arrived in Oakland, California, on June 6, she discovered to her surprise—and to the considerable disappointment of her sponsors—that

Miller had finished his coast-to-coast Autogiro trip the day before she left.

She immediately headed back, hoping to salvage the situation by setting the west-to-east transcontinental Autogiro speed record. But her trip home did not go smoothly, and on June 11 she crashed during takeoff in Abilene, Texas, damaging the rotors and hitting two cars. She returned home by train, claiming she'd been hit by a twister. On a later tour, while attempting to land at the Michigan State Fair in Detroit, she looped over, destroying the rotors of her Autogiro before a horrified crowd of onlookers. She privately admitted that she didn't think much of the machine. Publicly, however, she predicted in an article for *Cosmopolitan* magazine, "Your next garage may house an Autogiro," and claimed that

LEFT: *A poster announcing a promotional appearance. Earhart distributed Beech-Nut gum to the crowds at each stop on her transcontinental tour.*

BELOW: *The Beech-Nut Autogiro, nose down, after Amelia Earhart crashed on takeoff in Abilene, Texas, June 11, 1931.*

A roadable Autogiro.

the day was fast approaching when country houses would have wind cones flying from their roofs to guide guests to the front yard landing area.

By 1932, Autogiro engineers had innovated "direct control," enabling the pilot to control the direction of flight by tilting the individual rotors. This advance eliminated the need for stubby wings, moving the Autogiro a step closer to roadability. In 1934, Pitcairn's team developed vertical-jump takeoff, whereby a burst of high-speed spin from the rotors powered a straight pop up into the air, after which the propeller moved the aircraft forward. For roadability, they added a separate motor to power the rear wheel (as in Tampier's *Avion-Automobile*), although the vehicle's top speed was an unimpressive 25 miles per hour. Nonetheless, the Development Section of the U.S. Bureau

of Air Commerce commissioned a simplified and enhaced version of the small-cabin C-30 Autogiro, with its reconfigured rotors and jump-start. Such a promising marriage of motorcar and autogyro led to imaginative depictions in popular magazines of a fantasized and gussied-up Autogiro as the sleek commuter/family Girocar, perfect for every suburban garage because it didn't need a runway to take off.

The Pitcairn company came up with the handsome AC-35 Autogiro, a drivable personal aircraft that was first flown on March 26, 1936. It was constructed of metal and fabric wrapped around a steel tube framework. The rotors folded neatly back for driving, and the entire machine fit easily into an average-size garage. For driving, the propeller was disengaged and power was transferred to the rear wheel. The company claimed that the AC-35 was so easy to fly that licensed pilots would need no special rotary-wing training.

On October 6, 1936, to demonstrate this new marvel, James G. Ray once again flew an Autogiro to Washington, D.C., landed in a downtown park, and then drove through city traffic to the entrance of the Department of Commerce, where he accepted an award for "an aircraft of greater utility."

But despite the public acclaim, autogyros didn't catch on. The principal reason was that helicopters were catching up. Igor Sikorsky (1889–1972) is credited with inventing the first helicopter to feature a modern helicopter design. By 1936, German helicopters, capable of flying at 75 miles per hour, with a range of up to 150 miles, were being demonstrated at Nazi rallies by the celebrity test pilot Hanna Reitsch. They rose slowly and dramatically and hovered above stadiums. While the helicopter's speed and range were not impressive compared with those of an airplane—or those of an autogyro, which could also jump into the air—a helicopter could hold a stationary position in the air and even fly

LEFT: *The redesigned roadable AC-35 arrives in Washington, D.C., and is converted for driving by company vice president James G. Ray.*

BELOW: *Ray drove his Autogiro to the Department of Commerce, where he received his award.*

The 1941 Autogiro at the apex of its jump.

backwards. The Pitcairn Autogiro flew nearly as fast as an airplane, could take off vertically, and could even fly at low speeds . . . but it couldn't hover.

American military experts saw the helicopter's potential advantage for airlifts and air reconnaissance and shifted funding away from the autogyro—while still taking advantage of technology and patents developed for the autogyro to catch up with German helicopter technology. Additionally, most people didn't understand how the autogyro worked and so didn't trust it, which could be another reason that it fell from favor. The loss of military funding meant that the autogyro (and its evolution toward a Girocar in every garage) would be moved to a technological back burner, where for many years it was pursued only by an enthusiastic few. Seventy years after his transcontinental flight, Johnny Miller, who was still flying at ninety-eight years of age, claimed that the Autogiro was the safest aircraft in history and the only inherently safe airplane.

Back in December 1936, Juan de la Cierva, who had continued to fund autogyro development on his own and might have successfully championed autogyros as safer than either airplanes or helicopters, died in the crash of a conventional airplane. Had the forty-one-year-old inventor been in an autogyro when the engine failed, he'd likely have floated safely to earth, overhead rotors twirling gently.

The roadable AC-35 was presented to the Smithsonian in 1950. Harold Pitcairn died mysteriously of a gunshot wound in 1960. In 1966, the Pitcairn family won a settlement of more than $33 million in a legal battle to establish that Harold Pitcairn's patents had substantially contributed to the success of the helicopter.

9

JOSEPH GWINN'S AIRCAR

Joseph Marr Gwinn Jr. (1897–1956) was a World War I aviator and, later, an engineer at Consolidated Aircraft Corporation. In 1935, he founded the Gwinn Aircar Company in Buffalo, New York, intending to manufacture a small airplane specifically designed for the average automobile driver. The result was the Gwinn Aircar, promoted as a foolproof airplane that was as affordable as a mid-priced car. The Aircar succeeded so admirably at approximating the convenience, comfort, and easy handling of an automobile that it has often been misidentified as a roadable. Some accounts have even described a procedure for unbolting the wing panels from each side of the plane and manually redirecting power to the wheels for driving.

The Aircar's easy-to-fly design coordinated the steering wheel with the rudder and ailerons for directional control in the air, which made flying the Aircar feel like driving a car. The company claimed that landing an Aircar couldn't be simpler: Just fly down and level off, and the Aircar would land itself. To take off, just drive full speed down the runway and push the pedal all the way to the floor, and up you'd go.

Because of the coordinated controls, it took about half as long to learn to fly an Aircar as it did to learn to fly a conventional airplane, making the Aircar

*The Aircar, with Gwinn (*LEFT*) and test pilots Nancy Harkness and Frank Hawks, 1937.*

The Aircar's interior was designed to resemble that of a conventional car so drivers would feel comfortable and confident, as if they were driving in the air.

simple enough that the average driver could own and operate it instead of a second car. Frank Hawks, veteran pilot, air racer, and vice president of Gwinn Aircar, boasted, "With only an hour or two of instruction, any average person, even the intelligentsia, can fly our ship. It will not spin. It will not stall." With its carlike interior and its two automobile doors with automobile door handles, the aircraft felt familiar. Double wings created enough surface area to allow for a wingspan of only 24 feet, small enough to fit in a three-car garage. However, the Gwinn Aircar's commercial appeal was not helped by its rather absurd appearance, which was compared to a pollywog or a pregnant guppy.

The Gwinn Aircar in flight.

What brought the Gwinn Aircar Company down was not the Aircar's bulbous look or the sort of rookie pilot's mistake it was designed to prevent. Instead, it was an error made by its number-one advocate, Frank Hawks, a famously skillful and experienced pilot. During a promotional flight with a prospective client on August 23, 1938, Hawks's Aircar snagged a power line that was obscured by trees at the edge of a polo field in East Aurora, New York. The Aircar burst into flames, killing both Hawks and his passenger. The Gwinn Aircar Company suspended production that same year.

Joseph Gwinn returned to his previous employer, Consolidated Aircraft (now known as Consolidated Vultee), where he continued his work on small planes. But his continued commitment to roadable airplane research led him to publish a depiction of the ideal prototype for the much-anticipated flying car. The existence of this drawing may have contributed to the misapprehension that the Aircar was an airplane designed for the road.

A second Gwinn Aircar prototype was reportedly still flying, but not driving, in 1945.

The death of Frank Hawks
on August 23, 1938, was big news.

10

BUCKMINSTER FULLER'S DYMAXION OMNIDIRECTIONAL HUMAN TRANSPORT

Richard Buckminster Fuller (1895–1983) was a futurist philosopher, scientist, and designer who believed that twentieth-century technology had the potential to meet the needs of humankind without diminishing the planet. He is credited with coining the word *Dymaxion* from the phrase *dynamic maximum tension*—meaning "the most functional utility from a minimal material input." Buckminster, or Bucky (as his followers and friends called him), had no formal academic credentials, having been expelled (twice) by Harvard University, but he spoke with a professorial air when explaining his Dymaxion principle's potential to make the dream of

peace and plenty a modern reality in a Dymaxion world of tomorrow.

In 1928, Isamu Noguchi (1904–1988), a young artist who had just arrived in New York City from Paris, heard Fuller holding forth about his self-sufficient flying-saucer-shaped Dymaxion house. It was designed to be mass-produced and then lowered by zeppelin into any remote landscape. When asked, "Why a round house?" Bucky answered, "Why not!"

Noguchi was impressed with Fuller's "comprehensivist" vision, a creative fusion of design and science. Before long, the futurist and the modern artist were sharing an apartment in New York's Greenwich Village. Together they

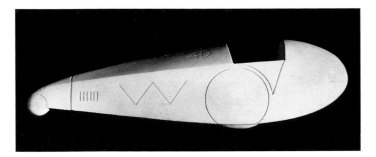

Isamu Noguchi's gypsum model for an "omni-medium transport" (Dymaxion car) sold at auction in 2008 for $92,500.

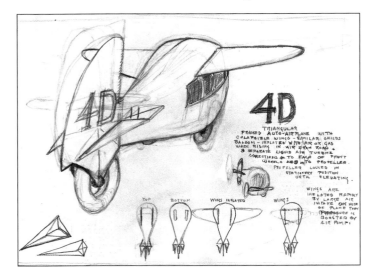

Fuller sketched a Zoomobile flying auto in 1928. It was designed to have inflatable wings and a propeller that would be locked when driving. Fuller called it his "4D twin, angularly orientable, individually throttleable, jet-stilt controlled-plummeting transport."

dreamed up an "omnidirectional transportation device," and Noguchi sculpted a streamlined plaster model, giving actual shape to their idea. Fuller's first sketch of a flying automobile, titled *4D Transport*, included inflatable wings and small jet engines. It was intended to carry passengers anywhere a Dymaxion house might be located. Fuller wrote to his daughter that a "Zoomobile," as she had called it, would be able to hop off the road at will, fly about, and then—as deftly as a bird—settle back into traffic.

The Fuller-Noguchi flying car never got off the ground. The proposed inflatable wings and the jet engines necessary for liftoff existed only on paper. But the concept was as revolutionary as any transportation device envisioned since Longobardi's combination vehicle.

Fuller rented an empty factory in Bridgeport, Connecticut, where he intended to build a practical automobile, without inflatable wings or jet thrusters but nonetheless based on up-to-date principles of airplane engineering. He and a small crew, led by the racing yacht builder Starling Burgess, constructed a 21-foot-long Dymaxion car prototype, resembling models built by Noguchi. Clad in sheet aluminum over a teardrop-shaped wooden frame and having a canvas roof, the Dymaxion car accommodated eleven passengers yet weighed less than 1,000 pounds. Its wide-set front wheels and unique centered-rear-wheel steering gave it a sensationally small turning radius, allowing it to be maneuvered into a seemingly impossibly small parking space.

The aerodynamic wooden framework of the first Dymaxion car.

Fuller claimed that the rear-mounted Ford V8 engine could power his lightweight, aerodynamic Dymaxion car at speeds up to 120 miles per hour, with a safe cruising speed of 100 miles per hour, while attaining gas mileage of 30–50 miles per gallon. (An ordinary 1933 Ford achieved about 16 miles per gallon.) However, the prototype showed a precarious instability, caused by the tendency of the single back wheel to leave the ground. But it was the Dymaxion car's bizarre appearance, not its instability, that earned it a stay-out-of-town order from the New York City police. While it was parked in front of Madison Square Garden, drivers stopped to stare, tying up traffic for hours.

Enthusiastic European manufacturers saw practical investment potential in Fuller's economical human transport prototype—that is, until the Dymaxion car collided tragically with a conventional automobile right in front of the en-

trance to the 1934 Chicago World's Fair. The prototype rolled over, its driver was killed, and two potential investors were injured. The Dymaxion car, now labeled the "Freak Auto" by the press, wasn't responsible for the accident, but manufacturing interest dried up anyway.

Fuller built one more prototype—this one for renowned orchestra conductor Leopold Stokowski, with a top fin for increased stability and a periscope in place of a rearview mirror. Celebrity pilot Amelia Earhart also ordered a Dymaxion car. But even such endorsements failed to reassure the public. Besides, Fuller had spent his entire inheritance to repair the second prototype and could not afford to build another.

Fuller foresaw a utopian society that would need lightweight, energy-efficient transportation combining the quickly evolving engineering principles of an airplane with the convenience of a car. Even if it didn't fly, his airplane car approached an engineering ideal of comfort and economy that is still pursued by twenty-first-century automotive engineers. He was one of the twentieth century's most celebrated futurists, inventors, writers, and lecturers, accumulating forty-seven honorary degrees. Yet to the end he remained an outsider, encouraging inventors to look past conventional wisdom and seek solutions unconstrained by historical limitations.

Noguchi and Fuller remained friends and collaborators until Fuller died on July 1, 1983, at the age of eighty-seven.

The shape of the Fuller-Noguchi Dymaxion car was echoed in the designs of Norman Bel Geddes, whose work also represented a combination of engineering and aesthetics. Bel Geddes began his career as a theatrical designer, and in 1929 he opened one of the first industrial design studios. He popularized the concept of streamlining, which is based on a teardrop shape and allows for smooth, efficient airflow.

Bel Geddes's 1945 concept for a flying car, named simply Flying Car, sported a rear propeller and extending wings. It was designed to satisfy the motoring public's desire to sit behind the wheel of an elegantly curvy sedan, whether on the road or in the air. But the art deco Flying Car was never produced, even as a prototype.

The Dymaxion car on display in the Chrysler pavilion at the 1934 Chicago World's Fair.
*At 20 feet—twice the length of a typical car—*Dymaxion Car 1 *always drew a crowd.*

WILLIAM BUSHNELL STOUT'S SKYCAR

As a child, William B. Stout (1880–1956) played with model airplanes made of cardboard and rubber bands. He went on to have a long career as an engineer and inventor, and among his many inventions was the first all-metal airplane, the Ford Tri-Motor. (At the time, conventional engineers still insisted that airplanes should be made of wood.) He also invented a self-propelled gasoline-powered railroad car called the Pullman Railplane, as well as movable theater seats and an air-cooled bed. Like Buckminster Fuller, Stout believed that successful design was improved by the judicious use of resources. "Simplicate and add more lightness" was, for him, the cardinal rule of engineering.

In 1912, Stout began publishing *Aerial Age,*

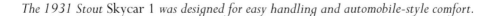

The 1931 Stout Skycar 1 *was designed for easy handling and automobile-style comfort.*

The 1932 Scarab car had no running boards, which allowed for a wider interior, and the engine was placed at the rear, eliminating the driveshaft bump. Other improvements included a smooth, aerodynamic body, four-wheel independent suspension, hidden door hinges, pushbutton door locks, and flush headlights.

the first aviation magazine in the United States. He was one of the reputable engineers in the late 1920s who believed that if small airplanes were designed so that piloting was as easy as driving a car, then flying would become part of everyday life. *Skycar I,* Stout's entry in the 1933 Easy Airplane Competition, was meant to make a driver-turned-pilot feel at ease when stepping into a plane. It was designed with a low door, like a car's, and a comfortably upholstered upscale interior. The instrument panel resembled the dashboard of an Oldsmobile, with key ignition, and the emergency brake and rudder pedals looked like a car's brake and clutch. Originally designed

for roadability, with a rear propeller protected by a steel tail assembly, the prototype was reconfigured with convenient hinged wings for ground maneuverability. Even so, the final prototype was never intended to double as a car, despite its misleading name.

Airplane design in the 1930s was miles ahead of automobile design in terms of efficiency and economy. In fact, according to some authorities, the average car was so unaerodynamic that it actually met less wind resistance going backward than it did going forward. Stout's streamlined Scarab car, named for the beetle sacred to ancient Egyptians, had four wheels and a turtle shape. Stout claimed the turtle was more stable than the teardrop favored by Fuller, and less apt to rise from the road—a characteristic, he pointed out, desirable in an airplane but not in a car.

The rear-engine Scarab car introduced innovations to auto making such as electric doors and controlled heating. By eliminating the running boards typically found on cars at the time, Stout made room for a wider interior, increasing the size of the luxurious passenger space, which featured leather, wood, and chrome. The Scarab's independent suspension allowed each wheel to react to a bump independently, making for such a smooth ride that only the driver's seat needed to be fixed in place. Passengers were free to arrange their seats however they chose—even at a table—and create a living room environment.

Only nine of the trendy Egyptian-style aluminum Scarab cars (and later, in 1946, the first fiberglass-reinforced plastic car) were produced. They sold for $5,000 apiece, the price of a new airplane at the time. One Scarab was said to have been purchased by a French businessman and later used as a mobile command post by General Dwight D. Eisenhower in North Africa during World War II. Eventually it housed monkeys in a circus. It was rescued and finally found a dignified home in a European automotive collection. Philip Wrigley (1894–1977), the chewing gum king, owned a Scarab car and used it as a beach car at his family's lakeside retreat until 1964. Five are said to

Movable furniture and a flat floor made the Scarab car's interior feel like a living room.

survive, including one in running condition at the Owls Head Transportation Museum in Owls Head, Maine.

Stout merged his company with Consolidated Vultee and brought along a model of a flying Scarab car with a removable flight module. The aircraft manufacturer was already enthusiastically hiring innovative engineers to design prototypes for a postwar flying car small enough to fit in a suburban garage, and Stout collaborated on the 1945 Spratt Stout Aircar. The Aircar made use of a removable "articulated wing" developed by George Spratt, which pivoted to adjust altitude and direction by means of a single control stick.

LEFT: *Bill Stout with a model of the Stout 1941 roadable Skycar, which had removable wings and twin tail booms, stainless-steel construction, and four-wheel landing gear.*

BELOW: *The* Convair 103 *(also known as the* 1944 Stout Skycar 4, *the* Spratt Controlwing, *and the* Flying Flea*) was successfully test-flown at Consolidated Vultee Aircraft Corporation's Stout Research Division.*

12

*T*HEODORE P. HALL'S CONVAIRCAR

World War II ended in 1945, and triumphant Americans imagined they were finally about to enter the "world of tomorrow." But instead of an environmentally conscious vision of optimal and careful use of resources for the good of humanity and the planet, they imagined a sprawling, mass-produced paradise with an abundance of techno-miracles, including scrumptious prepackaged meals served up by robotic appliances in the glistening kitchens of ultramodern push-button homes.

During the economic boom that followed World War II, victorious and newly affluent American consumers bought fully three-quarters of all the cars and appliances on earth. In such a buoyant climate, cheerful American motorists could easily believe in the possibility of a flying car in every garage. Congress had already discussed mandating the construction of runways alongside all new major highways, and *House and Garden* magazine was advising new homebuilders to "consider a landing strip as you would consider a driveway." All that was missing was the vehicle itself: a practical family car with wings.

Even before the postwar euphoria set in, Theodore P. Hall (1898–1978) had made his first attempt at designing a practical flying car, called simply the Roadable Airplane. Completed in 1939,

ABOVE: *Ted Hall's 1939 Roadable Airplane, a three-wheel automobile with a nose propeller. It never went into production.*

LEFT: *The first Roadable Airplane resembled a sporty convertible with a snout.*

it was powered by a V8 engine and looked like a three-wheel automobile with a snout and a propeller. Installing or removing its wings and divided tail required two technicians. Occasional sightings in the clouds in 1939 must have caused considerable astonishment. However, development never went beyond a prototype. When wartime priorities replaced civilian aircraft development, Hall accepted the position of design coordina-

tor for the B-24 heavy bomber, known as the Liberator.

In 1943, joined by his former Consolidated colleague Tommy Thompson, Hall resumed his quest to build the perfect postwar flying car. At the same time, to help raise money, he agreed to oversee the construction of the prototype being built in Garland, Texas, by Southern Aircraft. The SAC Aerocar looked more or less like a mid-1940s two-door sedan,

The 1946 SAC Aerocar, an experimental three-wheel flying car called the Roadable,

was said to be underpowered. It, too, never went into production.

but with three wheels and a protuberant attachment for a nose propeller. The gracefully divided tail and wings were removable, making it almost a normal-looking automobile on the street. In flight, the Aerocar was controlled by a combination of rudder pedals and a steering wheel that functioned like a joystick. In spite of encouraging performance and favorable publicity, the SAC Aerocar never went into production.

Back in San Diego, Hall resumed pounding aluminum sheets around a steel chassis using a rubber hammer. His prototype resembled a sort of slop-pily constructed Crosley, a sporty, lightweight war-era automobile originally sold in appliance stores. When outfitted with a sleek "flight module" powered by a 90-horsepower Franklin engine, it flew through the air like a car that had been snatched up by a mechanical albatross. In 1946, *Popular Science* magazine lauded Hall's convertible car-airplane as the most promising marriage between a small plane and an automobile.

Hall's ideas continued to develop, and he explained his new concept in his 1947 patent application for "Automotive Vehicles Adapted to Become Airborne by a

Novel Form of Flight Component." The design called for "complete independency of the flight component and its controls from the automotive unit" because "the interdependency of the control units in prior designs complicates the conversion of the vehicle from an airplane to an automobile and vice versa and obviously increases the possibility of failure and accidents due to improper rigging and malfunctioning of the controls." In other words, an independent flight module attached to a fully functional automobile would eliminate the problems that were caused by the complicated engineering adjustments necessary to combine an airplane with an automobile.

Back at Convair, executives and engineers were convinced that Hall's convertible car-airplane was exactly the postwar flying car they had been searching for. Convair agreed to invest in Hall's peculiar-looking vehicle and even fast-tracked further development at their main plant at Lindbergh field near San Diego. That made the newly renamed ConvAirCar the best-funded flying car venture ever undertaken.

Hall anticipated that flying car owners would drive their vehicles extensively on the roads, and so he equipped his new prototype with four wheels, not three. Meanwhile, Convair anticipated that Americans, with their love of glittering chrome and steel automobiles, were unlikely to be satisfied with a car that looked like a sheet-metal marshmallow, even one that could fly. So the company

In 1946, Ted Hall built a prototype of his own design for a flying car,
with an independent flight component and four wheels.

ABOVE: *With a slick redesign, the ConvAirCar 118 seemed a perfect fit for postwar suburban garages.*

INSET: *Independent flight component controls were designed to fit through the roof.*

turned to the renowned designer Henry Dreyfuss (1904–1972).

Dreyfuss, once a student of famed streamliner Norman Bel Geddes, was responsible for the modern look of many products from the 1930s to the 1960s, including the grand railroad train called the Twentieth Century Limited and the modest but ubiquitous Big Ben alarm clock. Dreyfuss, generally known as a practical thinker, agreed that a well-designed flying car would perfectly meet the modern expectations and transportation needs of affluent postwar suburban families. In that spirit, he designed a stylish yet respectable two-door, four-

passenger family sedan to be priced at $1,500, about the same as an earth-bound top-of-the-line Ford. Constructed of plastic impregnated with fiberglass, the new ConvAirCar weighed only 725 pounds and achieved an amazing 45 miles per gallon with a 24.5-horsepower Crosley engine.

The separate flight module consisted of a 190-horsepower engine, a single wing measuring 34.5 feet, a tail, a fuel tank, a propeller, and an instrument panel, all mounted on a spindly collapsible armature that attached right through the roof of the car.

Convair planned to rent the flight

LEFT: *Securing the flight component for takeoff . . .*

CENTER: *Taxiing . . .*

BOTTOM: *Airborne!*

modules to ConvAirCar owners at airports. The flight controls and gauges dropped cleverly into place over the pilot's head. The armature was then stowed neatly in wingtip access panels. On the ground at an airport or landing strip, the flight module could be detached from the automobile and jacked back onto its armature, and the ConvAirCar could be driven away, leaving the flight module behind. Traveling salesmen were considered the most likely customers. In the morning, a salesman could leave home, drive to the nearest airport, rent a flight module, fly hundreds of miles, land, remove the flight module, and drive to a business meeting in his prestigious-looking ConvAirCar. At the end of the day, he could return to the airport, re-attach the flight module, fly back to his home airport, remove the flight module and return it to Convair, drive to his house, and park in the family garage.

Convair executives projected impressive sales for the new ConvAirCar. They were confident that their revolutionary vehicle would appeal to a wide market: military pilots returning to civilian life as well as business travelers and weekend flyers. A ConvAirCar in the garage would be like having a car *and* an airplane, but without the storage and maintenance problems of owning two separate machines. "The market for this flying automobile will be far greater than any other conventional light plane," Convair announced confidently, "because a purchaser can obtain daily use from the car and get more from his investment." On November 17, 1947, the *New York Times* reported that a flying car had circled San Diego for an hour and eighteen minutes.

Hall had it right this time—the right styling and technology and also the right organization to put it into mass production. The ConvAirCar was a go!

But a few days later, on a routine test flight, something went wrong. Afterward, several explanations were offered: a gauge was broken, or a switch that should have been on was mysteriously turned off, or the test pilot mistakenly checked the ConvAirCar's gas gauge (which indicated adequately full) instead of the Convair flight module's aero fuel gauge (which was warning bone-dry empty). Whatever the reason, the ConvAirCar ran out of gas in midair. The test pilot managed to crash-land on a dirt road, but he shaved the wings off and totaled the fragile fiberglass automobile. Happily, he walked away. Sadly, he left more than just pieces of the handsome prototype strewn in the dust.

Some consider that the scattered auto and airplane parts near San Diego marked the end for flying cars. Even though the remaining prototype flew successfully, it was indeed the final act for Hall's marvelous ConvAirCar. Bad publicity after the crash wiped out Convair's corporate enthusiasm for flying cars, and the firm returned to the more predictably lucrative production of military planes. By 1948, after a quest lasting more than two decades, the most promising venture yet to mass-produce a flying automobile de-signed to meet the needs of a sprawling suburban postwar America had folded. The beautifully designed and functional ConvAirCar served instead as a cautionary tale, warning of the potential for calamity should ordinary drivers take to the sky in extraordinary cars.

In 1978, a fire at the San Diego Aerospace Museum destroyed the remaining prototype, but several scale models survive at the museum.

The test pilot survived this crash,
but Convair withdrew its support from ConvAirCar.

13

ROBERT FULTON'S AIRPHIBIAN

Twelve-year-old Robert Edison Fulton Jr. (1909–2004) was aboard the first scheduled airplane flight between Miami and Havana, Cuba, in 1920. Two years later, he was in the Valley of the Kings in Egypt when King Tutankhamen's tomb was opened. In 1932, at the height of the Great Depression, while Waldo Waterman, Robert Pitcairn, and Bill Stout grappled with the difficulties of designing an easy-to-fly airplane, Robert E. Fulton Jr., fresh from architecture studies at the University of Vienna, was attending fashionable dinner parties in London.

Over the clink of glasses and amid the cheery laughter one evening, "a pretty lady with toffee-colored hair" asked him if he would be sailing for home soon. Returning to New York by ship was his intention, so the answer he gave her took Fulton himself by surprise. "No," he said suavely. "I'm going around the world on a motorcycle!" Later he wrote, "I knew I'd done something inexplicably peculiar."

Also seated at the table that evening was Kenton Redgrave, the owner of Douglass Motorcycles, who chimed in, "I say there, that sounds grand. How about letting me furnish it?"

A few weeks later, Fulton was humming down the road astride a black Douglass Twin with gold stripes, a two-cylinder, six-horsepower engine tricked

In 1932, Fulton began his trip around the world on a Douglass motorcycle tricked out for documentary filmmaking.

out with two gas tanks, standard automobile tires (for easy replacement), a tool kit, and a hidden compartment containing a movie camera and film. After ferrying across the English Channel, Fulton rode through France, Germany, and Austria and on to Yugoslavia, where he discarded the formal evening clothes considered proper traveling gear for any respectable young gentleman.

Border guards frequently detained him, judging his intention to ride a motorcycle around the world as either crazy or just plain suspicious. But he persevered, charming his way past each checkpoint, and rode on. In Damascus, Syria, he was warned against attempting to cross the Blue Desert, some five hundred miles of sand and rock, alone. Unable to find a caravan that would allow him to ride along for safety, he loaded his motorcycle with all the extra water and gas it would carry. He drove the last ten miles of paved road to a weather-beaten sign reading BAGHDAD, with an arrow pointing across the open desert.

Fulton survived the crossing, but he spent seven weeks in a Baghdad hospital recovering from jaundice, locally referred to as "a desert chill on the liver."

Once restored to health, he motorcycled on through Afghanistan, India, Vietnam, and China. In Malaysia, he was offered a tiger cub. Even though assured that tigers make wonderful pets, he politely refused, explaining that "a motorcycle is no place for a baby tiger." From Japan he boarded a ship bound for San Francisco, then motorcycled eastward, arriving in New York City on Christmas Eve, 1933. Fulton claimed that his adventure gave him the courage to try many things and succeed.

He learned to fly a seaplane and became a successful aerial photographer. As war began to seem inevitable, he invented a much-needed training device to prepare aircraft gunners for modern air-to-air combat. His Gunairinstructor projected panoramic views of the sky based on movie footage he'd shot from the top of the Empire State Building. Sound effects simulated combat flying conditions. He enlisted other pilot trainers to fly to far-flung bases and teach military personnel how to best utilize the Gunairinstructor.

Fulton and his field instructors frequently found themselves stranded in desolate locations where local taxi drivers often refused to deplete their precious wartime gas rations by shuttling them to a remote military base and back again. "I'd end up kicking my airplane and say-

ing, why the %$@*& can't you take me down the road?" Fulton wrote later. His Stinson Reliant had all the necessary equipment—wheels, brakes, steering wheel, and engine—to drive to his destination, but without a way for him to separate the automobile parts from the airplane, he was stuck.

Fulton began working to solve the problem in the Washington, D.C., basement where he had developed the Gunairinstructor. Unobserved, he and nine associates welded, pounded, and wrapped fabric over steel tubes for more than eleven months. The airplane car they built was designed to leave its high-set wings and tail behind at an airfield, allowing the pilot to drive a road vehicle to his real destination. Once their craft was completed, they test-flew it in the dark near Middleburg, Virginia.

After the war, they secretly moved their project to Danbury, Connecticut, to a fifteen-acre plot next to the airport. Fearful that some shrewd aircraft manufacturer would steal his brainchild, Fulton test-drove the narrow two-seater convertible on deserted country lanes and flight-tested it at night, landing on a dark runway, rather than risk discovery. Finally, in 1946, Fulton's team publicly unveiled the Airphibian, to the praise of enthusiastic engineers and

The versatility of the Airphibian, an airplane that could leave its airplane parts behind to be driven like a car, was first demonstrated for the press in 1946.

readers of *Popular Mechanics* magazine. Two years later, they perfected a production prototype, suitable for presenting to the American driving public.

Life magazine featured photos of Robert and his wife, Florence, on an evening trip to the theater in New York City in their Airphibian. They flew at 110 miles per hour from Connecticut to LaGuardia Airport in Queens. There, Fulton himself detached the fuselage and the tapered wings and stored them in the airport hangar, and unbolted the propeller with a built-in wrench, all in less than five minutes. The right and left rudder pedals converted automatically to brake pedal and clutch. Fulton drove the convertible proudly into Manhattan at a breezy 55 miles per hour. The couple cruised down Broadway on four wide-set airplane tires and parked neatly outside the theater to attend a performance of the hit musical *Kiss Me, Kate.*

After the show, Fulton drove to the airport and backed the car up to the airplane flight component. He leveled the tail and wings to the proper height and cranked the supporting wheels into their storage position. Then he removed the prop spinner and the propeller from a bracket on the side and screwed the propeller into place with the built-in wrench. He secured the fittings, automatically engaging the instruments and

Life *magazine featured a photo-essay about the Fultons' trip to New York City for an evening at the theater.*

TOP LEFT: *Ready to go . . .*

TOP RIGHT: *Attaching the propeller . . .*

CENTER: *Approaching Manhattan . . .*

BOTTOM RIGHT: *Parking at the theater.*

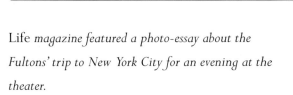

electrical connections, and locked them with three levers that held large pins in the fittings. The 150-horsepower, six-cylinder engine would not turn over for flight until every fitting was secured, but Fulton checked the warning light, just to be sure. The four-step conversion from automobile back to airplane took only five minutes, and the Fultons were soon on their way home to Connecticut through the clouds.

Eight production-model Airphibians were tested under different climatic conditions and in different geographical locations. Fulton drove and flew an Airphibian across the United States, Mexico, and Canada. His son Robert III, who often went along for the ride, learned to fly his father's car long before he could legally drive it. In response to the criticism that his car was too fragile, Fulton replied that no ordinary car was a match for his Airphibian's sturdy stability on the highway.

Fulton and his son Robert III, age three.

We had to test it until we beat it to death. A comment I have heard so often that it seems a cliché is that an airphibious vehicle can be "neither a good automobile nor a good airplane. It's a compromise." The argument is plausible but no more so than the fact that an ordinary automobile is also a compromise—it can't fly. An airplane likewise can't drive down

the road. In terms of pure transportation— a vehicle which will carry one the fastest the straightest, with the minimum of effort and expense yet with the maximum freedom of action and utility—the Airphibian is decidedly less of a compromise than any other vehicle.

In 1950, Fulton flew his production prototype Airphibian to Washington, D.C., and landed at National Airport. From there he drove it directly to the headquarters of the Civil Aeronautics Administration (later known as the Federal Aeronautics Administration) to claim the first official certification to begin production of a flying car in the United States. With more than 100,000 miles flown and 6,000 conversions successfully accomplished, the Airphibian was technically a great success. "This was a simple airplane," Fulton insisted, as well as "a simple little car that did the job very nicely."

However, Fulton's financial backers had become discouraged with the seemingly endless expense of meeting government production standards, and they withdrew their support. Unable to finance mass production himself, Fulton was forced to entrust a controlling interest in his project to a light-plane manufacturer, a situation he could not tolerate. Ironically, after all the secrecy to protect his inven-

tion from being stolen, the company that acquired the Airphibian decided that the much-anticipated postwar demand for personal airplanes wasn't materializing, and so it shelved the project. "At the time I felt very badly about it," Fulton wrote later, "but there is no use being unhappy about things; you simply accept the facts as they are."

Fulton filled his adventurous life with art, writing (including poetry and a pop-up book), and some seventy patented inventions. At the age of ninety-five, he still had the Douglass motorcycle, refurbished and ready to roll, parked in his garage.

The Airphibian is on view at the Smithsonian's Steven F. Udvar-Hazy Center in Chantilly, Virginia.

14

$\mathcal{D}$ANIEL ZUCK'S PLANE-MOBILE

The Vidal Safety Airplane Competition of the 1930s failed to produce the sort of flying flivver that many believed would lure millions of drivers into becoming pilots. And even when inexpensive secondhand planes—like the reliable, easy-to-fly Ercoupe—appeared on the market following World War II, few returning pilots or would-be weekend pilots rushed to buy them as predicted. Although inventor/engineers such as Hall and Fulton had successfully built prototype hybrid vehicles that eliminated the inefficiency of multivehicle travel, the inopportune crash of the sleek ConvAirCar and the commercial collapse of the marvelously functional Airphibian seemed to have

ended any hope for a practical flying car.

Even so, aeronautical engineer Daniel Zuck (1911–1992) and his partner Stanley Whitaker offered another solution in the form of a roadable, garage-sized airplane that stored its wings, insect-like, on top, which allowed it to be driven on the road like a car. Their Plane-Mobile (sometimes called a Plane-Auto), introduced in 1946, was begun in a San Diego workshop and later moved to Whitaker's garage in Los Angeles. It was designed with a push-pull steering wheel to control movement up and down as well as from side to side—like driving a car in three dimensions. "Two-control flying," as Zuck called it, coordinated rudder and

Daniel Zuck (LEFT) and Stanley Whitaker
pose with their invention.

ailerons, making safe turning automatic.

The innovative flexible wings, unlike the fixed wings of conventional aircraft, adjusted smoothly to air currents, preventing stalls and softening the ride like shock absorbers on a car. Ingenious airbrakes slowed the Plane-Mobile in flight, much like braking a car, for accurate landings. Zuck's design also limited the potential for steep dives in order to prevent users from indulging in the sort of barnstorming that required more skill than an inexperienced commuter pilot would likely possess. The Plane-Mobile

revived the tricycle design, with retractable wheels of the sort that engineers considered adequate for a roadable airplane.

Zuck's invention was designed unconventionally, even by flying car standards, to fly like a car and drive like a wingless plane. Admittedly, trying to use a Plane-Mobile as a conventional car rather than as a unique form of personal transportation would defeat its purpose. But the "floating wings" that adjusted to air currents and prevented stalls and spins had made the Plane-Mobile a finalist in the

1944 "Plane You'd Most Like to Own" contest in *Popular Science Monthly.*

The 1948 Cadillac was the first car to feature tail fins that resembled an airplane's. By the late 1950s, most automobile designs looked like flying machines. Zuck believed that the popularity of "airplanes without wings," as he called them, reflected a longing by motorists to convert grueling hours commuting on crowded highways to a daily adventure in the clouds. "The modern car," he wrote, "has slavishly imitated the airplane in almost everything except the wings. Why fly so low? Low flying is the most dangerous kind of flying. You already have an imitation airplane in your garage, so let's put wings on it and make the modern automobile fully functional, take the car off the road and fly where the flying is safe in the wide blue yonder." Zuck advocated using existing roads as runways for landing and taking off. In dangerous flying weather, of course, a pilot could fold his wings and drive on the roads instead.

In his self-published 1958 book, *An Airplane in Every Garage,* Zuck advanced an innovative vision that harked back to the optimistic predictions of future cities from the turn of the century. He foresaw driver/pilots commuting to reorganized downtowns that featured runways for landing and access streets

Zuck predicted that a Plane-Mobile parked curbside would become a commonplace sight in the suburbs.

that allowed roadable airplanes with folded wings to zip right to workplace parking lots. He also envisioned a more advanced Plane-Mobile, aptly called Advanced Model, with simple steering-wheel control rather than rudder pedals, and with power-operated automatically folding wings. "Auto building will become a lost art," he predicted, "replaced by personal airplane builders as soon as a worker can fly to work." As an added bonus, with no cars on the roads, "[traffic] congestion evaporates literally into thin air."

During the calamity of the Great Depression, Buckminster Fuller had envisioned a tranquil Dymaxion future with Dymaxion cars transporting happy modern families to prefabricated, self-sufficient Dymaxion houses. Zuck, in the postwar era of unprecedented affluence and optimism, predicted the opposite: an uncertain, fearful future shaped by the Cold War. His belief in an imminent nuclear attack by the Soviet Union added a unique urgency to his engineering quest for a flying car. In the 1950s, he wrote that his Plane-Mobile could provide the means to strategically scatter the population, thus denying the enemy congested urban centers as targets. In the event of a nuclear attack, driver pilots could scramble to

A roadable folding airplane that fit easily into an ordinary two-car garage would make a quick escape possible in the event of an attack.

evacuate threatened communities in their Plane-Mobiles. Far-flung suburban/rural Plane-Mobile commuters would already reside beyond the range of the initial impact and the radiation to follow. "Families will be far from dangerous military targets," Zuck assured his readers. "The threat of the hydrogen bomb to our lives and our homes will be minimized."

From the perspective of the twenty-first century, Zuck's plan to replace congested highways with a sky full of rush-hour commuters and his expectation that a population under attack would evacuate in their Plane-Mobiles seem naive. But his ideas must be understood in the context of backyard bomb shelters and "duck-and-cover drills," in which schoolchildren routinely practiced taking shelter under their desks as a defense against the effects of a hydrogen bomb. In the panicky atmosphere of the 1950s, converting roads to runways might be seen as a realistic solution. All it required was a small airplane that could be folded up and driven like a car, and Zuck had already invented one. "People will be able to take advantage of living in the quieter, less expensive country," he promised. "Peace and joy will surely follow."

Two prototypes of the Plane-Mobile were built and, until recently, were stored in a hangar in Palmdale, California. Another may be seen at the Mid-Atlantic Air Museum in Reading, Pennsylvania.

15

MOULTON B. TAYLOR'S AEROCAR

Moulton B. Taylor (1912–1995) was born at the right time for an aeronautical pioneer. Nine years earlier, the Wright brothers had motored 200 feet through the air. According to established aviation history (the Gustave Whitehead controversy notwithstanding), the Wright brothers' flight forever debunked the notion that flying machines were a fantasy. By the time Taylor began flying model airplanes with the Boy Scouts in the open fields west of Longview, Washington, real airplanes such as the Curtiss Jenny had proven their viability over the toxic trenches of Europe in World War I. And the price of a brand-new Ford flivver had dropped to below $300.

In 1926, Taylor watched barnstorming pilots roar out of the clouds and bounce their beat-up old Jennys and Hisso Standards across the bumpy field. The barnstormers were mostly experienced World War I pilots, and some adventurous women, too. They performed dangerous stunts in reconditioned (which often just meant repainted) biplanes bought at auction. Taylor sold tickets, leveled landing strips, pumped gas, and washed airplanes—likely in exchange for flying lessons, because on his sixteenth birthday he was ready to solo for a pilot's license. With some buddies, he bought an old Hisso Standard, and he flew it when he had gas money.

After college, Taylor entered Naval Aviation Cadet training. Later, in South America, he flew catapult-launched scout planes off cruisers.

In 1939, electronic navigational equipment, which used radio signals to guide aircraft when visibility was poor, was too expensive for small-plane owners. Taylor invented the Taylor AirPhone, a portable battery-powered navigational device. It attracted the attention of the navy brass, and Taylor was recalled into military service for a top-secret project. In 1942, he guided the first surface-to-surface missile to its target using a developing technology called television. The navy encouraged Commander Taylor to make weapons development his career, but Taylor declined. "I just decided not to spend the rest of my life making things to kill people," he said later. "I'm an idealist and admit it."

Taylor's ambition in 1946 was to manufacture a small sport plane with flotation wings, to be called the Duckling. That is, until he saw Robert E. Fulton Jr. and his widely publicized Airphibian. "I thought what a good idea, but I can do better," Taylor wrote later. He returned to an idea he'd sketched in 1945 and resolved to invent a vehicle that converted from airplane to automobile without leaving any parts behind.

His father, back in Longview, offered to help him find investors to finance his dream. Taylor suspected it might be a ruse to lure him home and talk some sense into him. Nonetheless, he convinced fifty business leaders to risk $1,000 each on his plan to build a flying car that would transport its driver and passenger as efficiently as an airplane but with the versatility of an automobile. "If the whole idea is to go where you please

Taylor's first sketch for a flying car.

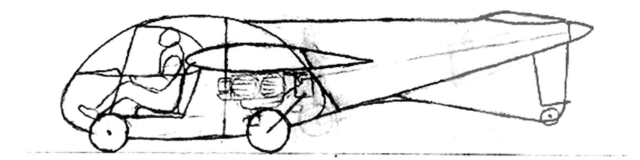

Taylor built this egg-shaped model to show investors.

when you please," Taylor asserted, "then leaving behind the flight components is a less than optimal solution."

Pilots would be able to land and drive through bad weather and take off again when the skies cleared. It was the same advantage René Tampier had promoted for his *Avion-Automobile* back in 1921. But Taylor was talking about a sporty little car, not a collapsible airplane that bumped down the street backward. Within a year, he promised, he'd drive an automobile to a nearby airstrip and then fly it back to Longview. He assured his investors that "the changeover from plane to automobile would be clean and easy enough for a woman in a fur coat with high heels."

Taylor built a modern-looking factory/ workshop beside a grass landing strip near the Columbia River. Where the

wall jutted artfully above the roof, he announced the name of his dream: Aero-car. He had not studied engineering—his university degree was in business—so he recruited two aircraft engineers, Charlie Kitchell and Art Robinson. Jess Minnick, an aircraft mechanic, was hired on too. He'd busted himself up back in 1919 after attaching wings to his motorcycle to see if it would fly. (It wouldn't.) Since then, he'd earned a reputation as a mechanical wizard who could fabricate anything. Taylor never took all the credit for the Aerocar. "There was no one person in charge of it and none of the parts were drawn up until we had something in hand," he said later, "so it was a kind of build and do."

The Aerocar team had many of the same objectives as "easy airplane" engineers in the Vidal competition of the early 1930s: a comfortable, automotive-style cabin with at least enough room for two adults and 100 pounds of baggage, flight controls as simple as a car's dashboard, and wide visibility.

Earlier engineers had designed small airplanes to fold or disassemble so that they could go for a short spin on the road. But a folding airplane, even a cool little Plane-Mobile, didn't meet Taylor's criterion of a genuine automobile with four automobile tires. He would create a brand-new breed of door-to-door vehicle, more practical than Robert Fulton's bouncy Airphibian and even Ted Hall's stylish ConvAirCar.

Taylor rejected the popular notion of a helicopter sedan. While helicopter cars have the theoretical advantage of backyard takeoff and thus require no runway, a helicopter displaces enough air to blow the shingles off a roof and flatten the flowers in the garden. "You can be sure your neighbors would never let you do it again," he said.

"We don't need a lot of complicated stuff, just a common sense gadget that will provide a usable practical little automobile and at the same time, unfold into a safe convenient airplane that you can drive over to the flying strip and fly to that other strip near Joe's place." So the Aerocar's design essentially fused an existing easy-to-fly airplane called the Ercoupe, dating back to the easy-airplane competition of the 1930s and admired for its proven reliability, to a lightweight utilitarian Crosley sports car. Produced between 1939 and 1952, the Crosley sold at appliance stores for as little as $250.

The Aerocar incorporated many features Taylor admired in the Airphibian's design, but he felt that watching the pilot screw the detachable propeller back on before takeoff might undermine passenger confidence in the aircraft's safety. However, he also knew that permanently mounted propeller blades would

A helicopter car in flight.

Taylor wanted to combine a reliable, easy-to-fly Ercoupe with an inexpensive, lightweight Crosley to create a flying sports car.

present a safety hazard on the street and that even a minor accident might make the propeller unsafe for flight. So the Aerocar team decided instead on a pusher (rear-mounted) propeller, like the one Waterman had used successfully for his Arrowbile. However, they positioned it at the end of a long cone so that the turbulent air it produced, called the propwash, would be left far behind the cabin. The cone angled upward for propeller-spin clearance and to keep the prop from whacking the ground on takeoff.

The engine, balanced in back of the cabin, vented exhaust and noise to the rear along with the unsettling propwash, making the Aerocar about as quiet and comfortable as an old Volkswagen Beetle. A Y-shaped tail, originally designed for a better fit in a suburban garage than a tall, thin tail, provided unexpected stability in the air. Acknowledging successful easy-to-fly airplane design elements dating from the 1930s, Taylor and his team positioned the Aerocar's wings high and back, giving the pilot/driver a wide, unobstructed view. The flight controls were linked so that the plane would bank and steer by means of the conventional automobile steering wheel. In flight mode, the wheel automatically accommodated itself to aileron control, so the pilot pulled it back to go up or pushed it forward to go down. Rudder pedals were added later, giving the pilot the option of conventional airplane controls. But unlike a conventional airplane's steering, the wheel swung back to center when released, like an automobile's. This automatically leveled the plane in the air, eliminating a dangerous mishap for inexperienced pilots: the inclination of conventional aircraft to continue a turn, if not corrected, into a spin called a Dutch roll or, more ominously, a graveyard spiral.

By the late 1940s, no respectable automobile came without headlights, parking and brake lights, a speedometer, an odometer, a good cabin heater with a three-speed blower, roll-down windows, windshield wipers, tinted sun visors, a radio, a rearview mirror, turn signals, a jack so the driver could fix a flat tire, a glove compartment, and a cigarette lighter and ashtray. The Aerocar had all of these features and also four-wheel independent suspension. The essential car horn doubled as a stall alarm. In the air, a flying car would also need airplane instruments: an airspeed indicator (in knots), an altitude indicator, a vertical speed (rate of climb) indicator, a compass, a turn and bank indicator, a hand throttle, a dual control stick, regulation flying lights, seat belts, a radio for use in flight, and a round airspeed indicator, clearly distinguishable from the long rectangular speedometer that

The Aerocar I's interior looked very much like the interior of a stylish compact car of its era.

Preparing to demonstrate his experimental Aerocar, Taylor arrived at the Aerocar factory on December 8, 1949, with a trailered flight component in tow.

showed ground speed. Yet by design the Aerocar's dashboard, instrument panel, standard gearshift, brake, gas pedal, and clutch closely resembled those found in any conventional late 1940s automobile.

Taylor's team decided against a two-engine modular vehicle, like the Conv-AirCar, in favor of a single engine with just one fuel gauge. The 143-horsepower Lycoming air-cooled aircraft engine they finally settled on gave the Aerocar a range of 500 miles in the air with a full forty-gallon tank. When the wings and tail were attached to the automobile, flight controls mechanically engaged by means of clusters of identical metal pads butting against each other. A lever in the cabin caused a particular pad in the cluster to

respond, affecting the rudder, ailerons, and elevators. The automatic matching up of clusters also disengaged the rear brakes, allowing the rear wheels to roll freely for landing, and popped the rudder pedals into position. Five pins locked the wings and tail in place. And if somehow a connection was still improperly fastened, a red warning light flashed in the center of the instrument panel. Like the Airphibian's engine, the Aerocar's engine would not start until every part matched up securely in place for flight, including the supporting wing struts. Under the dashboard there was a backup switch for double-checking that the warning light was functioning properly, just in case.

The primary innovation of the Aerocar

Driving into the sky.

that distinguished it from other proto-types, including Fulton's Airphibian, was that once the wing struts were disengaged, the wings folded smoothly back alongside the fuselage and tail, supported by small wheels (later made retractable). The entire flight compo-nent could then be rolled into a garage and left there, allowing the driver to zip around in a nifty-looking sports car. Or the fuselage, wings, and tail could be towed, trailer-like, and later reattached at another landing strip.

Just as Taylor had promised, *Aerocar I* was ready to roll on December 8, 1949. His backers—local businessmen, teach-ers, and doctors—gathered to see if their investment would fly. Taylor arrived for the trial run driving what was later de-scribed in the *Miami Herald* as "one of the ugliest automobiles ever put together. . . . But never mind," the article contin-ued. "Here's what Taylor would do; he'd drive this thing to the Kelso airport, put on the wings and fly back. That ought to prove the point, oughtn't it? Which it certainly did. The investors were over-joyed." Popular magazines proclaimed the Aerocar the transportation of the future. Taylor and his team doggedly continued perfecting the prototype. Jess Minnick described driving the Aerocar as "much like getting a good start on a drag strip with the difference that you just keep going, off, up and out over the crowd."

It took almost eight years and some seven hundred hours in the air, 20,000 miles on the road, and hundreds of structural tests before government inspectors at the Civil Aeronautics Authority unreservedly okayed Aerocar for mass production in December 1956. The Aerocar also complied with the motor vehicle codes in all the states that had them. An enthusiast wrote in 1957, "You can walk into the factory today, pay your money and drive out with a flying automobile. . . . With everything necessary for an airplane and a car, the interior has an attractive, uncluttered appearance. The Aerocar is fun to drive and gives a very acceptable jeep-like ride, with front-wheel drive and a top highway speed of 65." A popular rock and roller, Chuck Berry, sang its praises in a song called "You Can't Catch Me."

Taylor launched an all-out campaign to attract a backer for his newly government-approved Aerocar: an aircraft corporation or, better yet, an automobile manufacturer already geared up for much larger production. He sold three hand-built experimental prototypes for $15,000 each and used the proceeds to begin tooling up Aerocar Co. for mass production. He made public appearances with his creation across the country, including one on the popular television game show *I've Got a Secret*. His secret, of course, was "I flew to New York in this automobile." But no company stepped forward.

Mrs. Taylor, out grocery shopping in Aerocar I.

Taylor's redesign of the Aerocar
was based on a toy Jaguar.

The Bob Cummings Show, another popular television show in the early 1960s, featured a soaring Aerocar in its opening sequence. Bob Cummings said his new car "could really give you a lift." Unfortunately, the show's sponsor, vitamin manufacturer Nutri-Bio, came under investigation for making dubious advertising claims, and Aerocar's precious national exposure came to an abrupt end. The fortunate sons of a hamburger entrepreneur in Illinois became the proud owners of that particular Aerocar. They drove it back and forth to high school every day—but never flew it.

For a few years, an Aerocar circled over Portland, Oregon, doing the traffic reports for radio station KISN. "Knows the traffic, 'cause it's been there!" the announcer boasted. Throughout those years of daily service, the Aerocar required only routine maintenance.

Impressed with the Aerocar's performance, a light airplane company in Fort Worth, Texas, offered to begin production in 1961, as soon as Taylor guaranteed five hundred firm orders. The Associated Press announced that a contract had been signed and that it wouldn't be long before a thousand Aerocars a year were rolling out the door, ready to take off, available for purchase at $8,500 apiece.

Taylor had long proclaimed, "The public is begging for a flying automobile." He was on his way to holding up his end of the deal when the company suddenly informed him that the money needed for tooling up the factory was gone. It had been squandered by the sales organization formed to promote and facilitate Aerocar sales even before adapting the factory for production had begun. Colossally disappointed, Taylor watched his best chance collapse.

But disappointment didn't stop him. "As for me losing sleep," he said, "I quit doing that a long time ago. . . . I just keep trying." When one of the original five hand-built Aerocars was returned to the Aerocar factory, having been badly damaged in a road accident, Taylor and Jess Minnick decided that instead of simply repairing it, they would redesign and update its 1945 styling, using a toy Jaguar as their model. *Aerocar III,* completed in 1968, looked like a slick European sports car. Its new interior resembled that of the popular Ford Mustang, with "such niceties as bucket seats and soundproofing." New fender wells accommodated automobile tires that lowered for landing and takeoff, retracted to an intermediate driving position for the road, and pulled up into the fenders to decrease drag and increase air speed in flight. Asked how long it would take to convert the sleek new *Aerocar III* to a plane, Taylor answered, "Less time than it takes to carry your bags from your car to your airplane."

The December 1969 issue of *Flying* magazine complimented *Aerocar III* on its sports-car good looks, and added, "It is also quick and comfortable; and when Molt Taylor hurls it across the railroad tracks at 80 mph, holding both hands in the air, you are convinced that it has remarkable handling qualities. It's not so quiet as a Cadillac, but what sports car is?"

In 1970, the president of Ford Motor Company, Lee Iacocca, ordered a feasibility study of the market potential for a mass-produced Ford Aerocar. The study estimated likely sales of 25,000 a year. This was no surprise to Taylor, whose faith in the Aerocar was unwavering. "Flying automobiles would provide far greater use potential than any other single vehicle," he'd written of his *Aerocar III,* "giving door-to-door transportation at a speed and convenience never offered

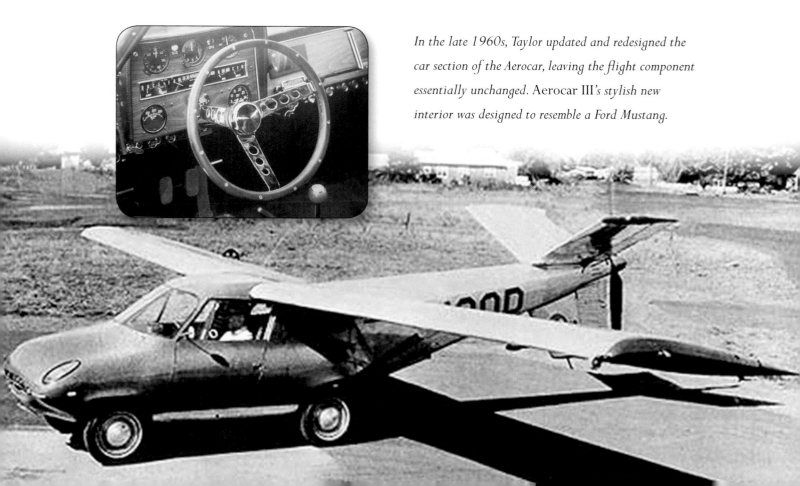

In the late 1960s, Taylor updated and redesigned the car section of the Aerocar, leaving the flight component essentially unchanged. Aerocar III's stylish new interior was designed to resemble a Ford Mustang.

Aerocar III, *flying with retracted wheels.*

before by making the freeways of the air available to everyone."

But officials at the Department of Transportation were aghast at the notion of thousands of commuters flying over large population centers. Taylor protested that existing air traffic systems could handle small planes as easily as the highways accommodated cars. "The only reason somebody can drive from New York to Florida," he fumed, "is because some stupid guy walked down the road ahead of you and drew a yellow line in the middle of the road." He insisted that every plane in the United States, including airliners, could be arranged in the air over Washington State so that no one in

any plane would be able to see another airplane. "So don't tell me that the skies are crowded!"

Unconvinced, executives at Ford worried that such a bold innovation might become a costly industrial joke at their company's expense. The engineers claimed that compliance with new government automobile safety regulations would add so much additional bulk to the Aerocar that it would be unable to fly, thus reviving the weight-versus-efficiency argument that had been leveled against flying cars from the beginning.

America was no longer a wide-open country with few roads braved only by the most intrepid motorists and flown over by visionaries like Glenn Curtiss. The nation had built an efficient system of highways that connected an ever-increasing number of population centers. Most drivers, it turned out, were content to remain make-believe pilots behind the wheel of streamlined airplane-shaped cars, driving at takeoff speed on well-engineered, comfortable roadways. The handsome, efficient *Aerocar III,* which had made "little if any compromise with either conventional light planes in their weight power class, or automobiles that can't fly," landed once and for all in the Museum of Flight in Seattle.

Taylor had innovated right to the limits of twentieth-century imagination, but it seemed the postwar window of opportunity for flying cars had closed, and even his capacity for reinvention couldn't re-open it. Levelheaded, sensible officials at the Department of Transportation concluded that there was no such thing as a foolproof flying car and that in any case, it would be wiser not to tempt foolish drivers to fly.

But Taylor wasn't quite finished. The small amphibious sport plane he'd set out to build after the war, renamed the Coot, was reborn in 1989 in the form of a "homebuilt"—a do-it-yourself kit. While redesigning the Coot for home

Taylor proposed converting a lightweight Honda CRX into a flying car with a powered flight component.

assembly, Taylor got to thinking, "If the DOT [Department of Transportation] won't let us certify our airplane as a car, we'll approach it from the other direction. We'll take a car that's already certified and make it into an airplane!" He designed a similar kit for a self-powered flight component to take advantage of the same federal loophole that allowed hobbyists some legal leeway to experiment with small airplane building. "People go out and buy the car," explained Molt. "We send them the plans and materials, and they put it together themselves." He planned to convert a popular Honda CRX for driving the infinite highway of the air.

16

$\mathcal{I}$NTO THE FUTURE

In 1959, seventeen-year-old Ed Sweeney got a flying lesson in an Aerocar from Molt Taylor. "It's easy," Taylor told him. "It practically flies itself. I'll tell you what to do as we go along."

Ed Sweeney didn't stop there. In 1988, he bought a 1956 Aerocar prototype. Then, inspired by Taylor's homebuilt

Aerocar 2000.

designs, he devised the slick, modular Aerocar 2000. He combined a $30,000 Lotus Elise with a built-on interface for an independent flight component to be constructed by the buyer from a kit consisting of FAA-approved parts. Thus, he abandoned Taylor's fundamental innovation—towing the wings. This was to take advantage of a legal loophole that allowed flying cars that were 51 percent homebuilt. The entire flying car, including the two-seat roadster, had been projected to sell for $100,000, but flight testing was never completed. Mr. Sweeney and his son reportedly were still flying and driving their *Aerocar 1* to air shows at the time of this writing.

The computerized, autonomous navigation technology that will make it possible for anyone to drive or fly is not yet legal or marketable. In the meantime, advocates insist that even using available technology, flying cars would greatly reduce the routine mayhem of automotive travel. They point out that while many small planes are flown safely every day, there are thousands of automotive fatalities every year.

Terrafugia is a private Massachusetts-based company founded by graduates of the Massachusetts Institute of Technology. They claim that their two-passenger Transition, which is priced at $287,000, transforms in thirty seconds from a car to an airplane. There is information about reserving your own flying car, with just a $10,000 refundable deposit, on the Terrafugia website.

The three-wheel PAL-V ONE is a sporty two-seat hybrid car and gyro-

The PAL-V ONE, a two-seat hybrid car and gyroplane, is designed to provide door-to-door transportation.

plane that requires very little space for takeoff and landing. It can be driven to the nearest airfield, where the propeller is unfolded for flight. An automatically folding rotor is still in development, but the propeller folds itself on landing. A button lowers the rotor mast into the horizontal position. Gyroplanes characteristically take off and land at low speed, cannot stall, and can be landed safely even if the engine fails because the unpowered rotor keeps rotating. The Dutch company PAL-V Europe NV has successfully conducted test flights.

The dual-mode Carplane being developed at the Research Airport in Braunschweig, Lower Saxony, Germany, when this was written, will be a hybrid two-passenger vehicle, designed to convert at the touch of a button from an electric-

Terrafugia Transition,
New York International Auto Show, 2011.

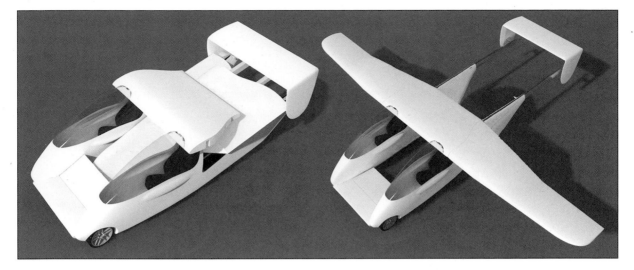

The Carplane road/air vehicle is designed to transform from car to plane in fifteen seconds.

powered road car to an internal combustion–powered plane with a cruising speed of 136 miles per hour.

In the early 1950s, the U.S. Army experimented with a revolutionary hovering platform that was propelled by contra-rotating five-foot-wide rotors. These versatile vehicles proved surprisingly stable, but their powerful engines required a great deal of maintenance. The early military prototypes also made slow-moving targets. In the late 1950s, helicopter manufacturer Frank N. Piasecki (1919–2008) developed the Piasecki Air Jeep, which flew with the adaptability of a helicopter and was capable of hovering

The basic design of the 1958 Piasecki Air Jeep featured two large rotors at the front and back of the craft.

a few feet off the ground using ducted-fan technology and of rising several hundred feet into the air. The Piasecki Air Jeep's vertical takeoff and landing technology opened another possible avenue for the development of a flying car, since vehicles with enclosed rotors, unlike those with whirling helicopter blades, could safely be driven in traffic.

Paul Moller's Skycar, in development for more than thirty years, can take off nearly straight up from a driveway. The tradeoff, however, is that eight rotary engines are required to create the nearly 1,000-horsepower force needed (compared with the 143-horsepower engine that powered Taylor's first Aerocar off a landing strip). According to moller.com, Moller's Skycar 400, projected to fly at almost 400 miles per hour, was under testing when this book was written.

The Defense Advanced Research Projects Agency has revolutionized the concept of a flying car by creating the

LEFT: *Paul Moller's Skycar.*

BELOW: *The Transformer TX.*

CityHawk.

Transformer, an unmanned aerial system. Lockheed Martin's Skunk Works is leading a team with Piasecki Aircraft to build autonomous flying wings, configured to attach to an earthbound Humvee and convert it to a GPS-controlled flying car small enough to drive along a single-lane road. The Transformer will be able to make unpiloted trips with supplies into places inaccessible by road. It will have a smaller landing zone than a standard helicopter, thanks to tilting ducted fans, which will also make it faster and safer.

Rafi Yoeli, an Israeli inventor, constructed a 1,200-pound prototype of the two-seater CityHawk flying car in his Tel Aviv living room. After founding Urban Aeronautics Ltd. in 2001, he turned his attention to a hovering vehicle intended for police and rescue use. Even some who doubt the practical viability of a flying car concede the potential of a versatile hybrid urban rescue vehicle or a roadable flying ambulance where roads are scarce or perilous. CityHawk would be able to rescue people trapped inside high-rise buildings by hovering close enough to a window that a person could step onto the platform. Hundreds of tiny adjustable slats at the edge of two encased horizontal fans,

ABOVE: *A recent model.*

INSET: *Vernon Porter and Clarence Kissell in their workshop in Murphy, Texas,*
with a fiberglass mockup of their original GT flyer.

each powered by four internal combustion engines, make possible instant directional changes and the flexibility to rise from just inches off the ground to 12,000 feet in the air. It features a ducted fan design requiring no runway; is capable of operating even on a crowded street; and can be used as a taxi, an ambulance, a bridge inspection vehicle, and, eventually, even a family car.

On April 1, 2007, the *Dallas Morning News* ran a story about Dr. Vernon Porter, age seventy-two, and Clarence Kissell, age seventy, who were building a flying car with their own hands in a workshop behind Dr. Porter's house. Several prototypes later, their three-wheel (two wheels in front, one in back) vehicle was constructed of fiberglass and foam, so although it's as wide as a minivan and as long as an SUV, it weighs only 1,200 pounds—2,000 with gas and a passenger. A GM six-cylinder engine will power it both on the ground and in the air. The wings will fold back neatly into slots for driving.

Dr. Porter asserts, "It should drive and fly pretty well."

And Mr. Kissell remains optimistic. "We think it will work."

AUTHOR'S NOTE

In 2002, I read an article in the Driving section of the *New York Times* about Molt Taylor's 1949 Aerocar, a funny-looking but oddly appealing little automobile with a flight-conversion option. Taylor thought that the technology for automatically converting the family car to an airplane could be as simple as raising and lowering a mechanical convertible top with the press of a button.

The notion of a flying car parked in every garage struck me as the best/worst idea ever. Cars break down and drivers miscalculate and make mistakes that are catastrophic enough even when they don't happen overhead. Still, think about pressing a button and transforming your car's trunk to a tail with a spinning propeller . . . about telescoping wings that extend and click into place overhead . . . about pulling back on the steering wheel and driving right into the sky!

Whether it was a brilliant idea or a colossally bad one, I had discovered that a flying car isn't just a commuter's daydream or a rollicking tall tale for the modern age. I saved the article about the heroic little car that seemed to defy common sense and stashed it in my sketchbook.

By the time I unfolded the yellowed newspaper article about Taylor's dream car and reread it, I'd discovered that Taylor wasn't the first inventor to build a flying car. He was one in a still-unfolding long line of visionaries. Their timeline extends back to Gustave Whitehead in 1901 and Trajan Vuia in 1906, and continues forward, with the speed of digital innovation, to prototypes such as the Carplane and PAL-V ONE. Each prototype is a testament to the unfaltering belief that the real compromise is being restricted to driving cars that can't fly.

I have tried to convey the enthusiasm of inventors who felt certain that they had devised the right prototype at just the right historical moment to successfully introduce automobile drivers to flying cars. To maintain the story's momentum, I've left out some worthy efforts. One of the most notable was the 1971 AVE (Advanced Vehicle Engineers) Mizar, a combination Ford Pinto and Cessna Skymaster built by Henry Smolinski and Harold Blake. On September 11, 1973, just months before production was scheduled to begin, the right wing detached and the Pinto plummeted to earth, killing them both. Though the innovative use of a mass-produced automobile was so promising that the Mizar nearly went into production, I decided that the malfunction and resulting deaths unnecessarily repeated the pattern of flying cars as a cautionary tale.

Despite tragic headlines, rational critics, skeptical insurance companies, and nervous homeowners, flying car inventors and enthusiasts pursue their engineering ideal, pinning their hopes on new computer navigation technology that reacts faster than humans and doesn't get distracted, sleepy, or intoxicated. An autonomous Toyota Prius developed by Google has reportedly been driving itself safely around San Francisco, with human supervision, since 2010. Autonomous vehicle technology is being developed for flight as well. Once the Pentagon unveils an automated aerial system to convert a Humvee for flight, can a family car transformed for computerized flight be far behind?

GLOSSARY

aeronaut aviator; originally referred to a balloonist.

ailerons tilting surfaces in a plane's wings that make the plane roll to one side or the other.

airplane a self-powered heavier-than-air flying machine.

airship a lighter-than-air aircraft with a steering mechanism.

altitude height above sea level.

angle of attack the angle at which a wing meets the wind.

biplane a plane with two sets of wings, one above the other.

bumper a metal or rubber barrier at either end of a motor vehicle, meant to absorb impact in a collision.

elevators tilting surfaces on a plane's tail that make the plane dive or climb.

fixed-wing aircraft aircraft with wings that do not move.

flying wing a plane with no tail, shaped like large wings.

fuselage the main body of a plane.

glider an unpowered fixed-wing aircraft.

Global Positioning System (GPS)
a navigation system for locating a position accurately using radio signals from satellites.

landing gear an aircraft's wheels.

lift an upward-acting force produced by wings, rotor blades, engine thrust, or a lighter-than-air gas.

lighter-than-air craft an aircraft kept aloft by a large gas bag lighter than the surrounding air.

monoplane a fixed-wing aircraft with one wing across the top or one wing on each side.

navigation steering a course.

pitch movement of an aircraft that tilts the nose up or down.

radar a system for locating aircraft by sending out bursts of radio signals and detecting reflections that bounce back.

retractable wheels wheels that fold up inside the aircraft.

roll the banking movement of an aircraft in which one wing rises and the other falls.

rotor a set of rotating blades.

rudder a control surface in an aircraft's tail fin that swivels left or right to turn the plane in a particular direction.

seaplane a plane with floats that allow it to land on water, sometimes called a float plane.

spin an aggravated stall resulting in a corkscrew downward path.

stall a loss of lift that occurs when an aircraft is flown at an angle of attack greater than the angle for maximum lift. If recovery from a stall is not achieved quickly by reducing the angle of attack, a secondary stall and a spin may result.

SOURCE NOTES

CHAPTER 2
Gustave Whitehead's Condor

6   "more or less successful": www.gustave-whitehead.com.

8   "That was . . . like it": www.gustave-whitehead.com.

CHAPTER 3
Trajan Vuia's Aéroplane-Automobile

11–12   "The problem . . . dream": Trajan Vuia at www.ctie.monash.edu.au/hargrave/vuia.html.

12   "The flying . . . 10 million years": "Flying Machines Which Do Not Fly" (*New York Times,* October 9, 1903), quoted in Moolman, *Road to Kitty Hawk,* 149.

     "I have . . . two wings": Trajan Vuia at www.ctie.monash.edu.au/hargrave/vuia.html.

14   "Vuia Airplane . . . Flight": Trajan Vuia at www.ctie.monash.edu.au/hargrave/vuia.html.

16   "1906 . . . France": Stiles, *Roadable Aircraft,* n.p.

CHAPTER 4
Glenn Curtiss's Autoplane

20   "Now if . . . have something!": C. E. Glass, "The Personal Aircraft—Status and Issues," NASA Technical Memorandum 109174 (1994), 9.

CHAPTER 5
Felix Longobardi's Combination Vehicle

26   "There are . . . build them": Alice Fuchs, "Report on the Aerocar," *Flying* (September 1957), 57.

CHAPTER 6
Henry Ford's Flying Flivver

30   "Small enough . . . office": Bob Blake, "Time Was," www.aaca.org/publications/ rummagebox/2005/spring/spring05c.htm.

"Mark my words . . . will come": Bob Sillery, "A Plane-Car for the Man of Average Means," *Popular Science* (March, 2000), 74.

CHAPTER 7
Waldo Waterman's Arrowbile

31   "Now if . . . have something!": C. E. Glass, "The Personal Aircraft—Status and Issues," NASA Technical Memorandum 109174 (1994). 9.

32   "a flying tool shed": James R. Chiles, "Flying Cars Were a Dream That Never Got Off the Ground," *Smithsonian* (February 1, 1989), 146.

CHAPTER 8
Harold Pitcairn's Autogyro

37   "Inventor Cierva . . . aviation": Leon Clemmer, *Horsham Township* (Charleston, S.C.: Arcadia, 2004), n.p.

40   "Your next . . . Autogiro": Bruce H. Charnov, "Amelia Earhart, John M. Miller and the first Transcontinental Autogiro flight in 1931" (unpublished paper delivered at Hofstra University, February 2003). www.aviation-history.com.

CHAPTER 9
Joseph Gwinn's Aircar

46   "With only . . . stall": "Frank Hawks and the Gwinn Aircar," www.check-six.com/ Crash_Sites/Gwinn_Aircar-Hawks.htm, 2002.

CHAPTER 10
Buckminster Fuller's Dymaxion Omnidirectional Human Transport

48   "Why . . . not!" Doug Yurchey, "Buckminster Fuller—the World Is Round?" www. hiddenmysteries.org/index.html.

49   "Zoomobile": Michael John Gorman, "Dymaxion Timeline, 1927," hotgates.stanford. edu/Bucky/dymaxion/timeline.htm, 2002.

50   "Freak Auto": Patrick Cooke, "Sappy Motoring," *Forbes FYI* (Spring 2001), 73.

CHAPTER 11
William Bushnell Stout's Skycar

52   "Simplicate and . . . lightness": J. A. Greenberg, "William B. Stout and His Wonderful Skycar," *Mechanix Illustrated* (November 1943), 45. Whether Stout invented this phrase or adopted it is not known, but engineers have been quoting it ever since.

CHAPTER 12
Theodore P. Hall's ConvAirCar

56   "consider a landing strip . . . driveway": James R. Chiles, "Flying Cars Were a Dream That Never Got Off the Ground," *Smithsonian* (February 1, 1989), 150.

59   "complete . . . controls": Stiles, patent # 2,562,491, n.p.

62   "The market . . . investment": William Gurstelle, *Adventures from the Technological Underground: Catapults, Pulsejets, Rail Guns, Flamethrowers, Tesla Coils, Air Cannons, and the Garage Warriors Who Love Them* (New York: Three Rivers Press, 2006), 16.

CHAPTER 13
Robert Fulton's Airphibian

64   "a pretty lady . . . hair": Fulton, *One Man Caravan*, 5.

65   "a desert . . . liver": Fulton, *One Man Caravan*, 79.

66   "a motorcycle . . . tiger": Fulton, *One Man Caravan*, 207.

      "I'd end up . . . road?": quoted in Andrea Zimmerman, "Invention in All Its Beguiling Varieties," *New York Times* (March 8, 1998), archived, www.nytimes.com/1998/invention-in-all-its-beguiling-varieties.

69   "We had to . . . vehicle": Shultz, *A Drive in the Clouds*, 99.

70   "This was . . . very nicely" and "At the time . . . they are": quoted in Andrea Zimmerman, "Invention in All Its Beguiling Varieties," *New York Times*, (March 8, 1998), archived, www.nytimes.com/1998/invention-in-all-its-beguiling-varieties.

CHAPTER 14
Daniel Zuck's Plane-Mobile

71   "Two-control flying": Zuck, *An Airplane in Every Garage*, 97.

72   "floating wings": Zuck, *An Airplane in Every Garage*, 99.

73   "Plane You'd Most Like to Own": *Popular Science Monthly* (September 1944), quoted in Zuck, *An Airplane in Every Garage*, 163.

      "The modern . . . yonder": Zuck, *An Airplane in Every Garage*, 45.

74   "Auto building . . . work": Zuck, *An Airplane in Every Garage*, 123.

      "[traffic] . . . air": Zuck, *An Airplane in Every Garage*, 123.

75   "Families . . . minimized": Zuck, *An Airplane in Every Garage*, 125.

      "People will . . . follow": Zuck, *An Airplane in Every Garage*, 125.

CHAPTER 15
Moulton B. Taylor's Aerocar

77   "I just decided . . . admit it": quoted in Shultz, *A Drive in the Clouds*, 2.

      "I thought . . . better": quoted in John Grossman, "What Has Four Wheels and Flies? The Dream of the Roadable Airplane," *Air & Space* (January 1996), n.p.

77–78   "If the whole . . . solution": quoted in Powell, "Winging It," n.p.

78   "the changeover . . . high heels": quoted in Shultz, *A Drive in the Clouds,* 23.

    "There was . . . and do": quoted in Shultz, *A Drive in the Clouds,* 39.

79   "You can . . . again": quoted in Shultz, *A Drive in the Clouds,* 49.

    "We don't need . . . Joe's place": quoted in Shultz, *A Drive in the Clouds,* 25.

83   "one of the . . . overjoyed": Powell, "Winging It," n.p.

    "much like . . . the crowd": Jess Minnick, "Flying Cars Are Here!" *Motor Trend* (December 1951), 15.

84   "You can walk . . . speed of 65": Alice Fuchs, "Report on the Aerocar," *Flying* (September 1957), 39.

    "I flew . . . automobile": *I've Got a Secret,* October 18, 1959. www.youtube.com/watch?v=WiFjhw_Iq9s.

85   "could really . . . lift": quoted in Shultz, *A Drive in the Clouds,* 62.

    "Knows . . . been there!": quoted in Shultz, *A Drive in the Clouds,* 65.

    "The public . . . automobile": quoted in Shultz, *A Drive in the Clouds,* 14.

    "As for me . . . keep trying": quoted in Shultz, *A Drive in the Clouds,* 58.

86   "such niceties . . . soundproofing": quoted in Shultz, *A Drive in the Clouds,* 72.

    "Less time . . . airplane": Robert Blodget, "The Taylor Aerocar (Remember the Taylor Aerocar?) Is Alive and Well in the Air and on the Road," *Flying* (December 1969), 54.

    "It is also . . . car is?": Powell, "Winging It," n.p.

86–87   "Flying automobiles . . . everyone": *Aeromagazine* (November–December 1968), 54.

87   "The only . . . of the road": quoted in Powell, "Winging It," n.p.

    "So don't . . . crowded!": quoted in Powell, "Winging It," n.p.

88   "little if any . . . can't fly": Robert Blodget, "The Taylor Aerocar (Remember the Taylor Aerocar?) Is Alive and Well in the Air and on the Road," *Flying* (December 1969), 54.

    "If the DOT . . . an airplane!": Powell, "Winging It," n.p.

    "People go . . . themselves": Powell, "Winging It," n.p.

CHAPTER 16
Into the Future

89   "It's easy . . . go along": John Grossman, "What Has Four Wheels and Flies? The Dream of a Roadable Airplane Continues," *Air and Space* (January 1996), n.p.

94   "It should . . .well" and "We think . . . work": Terry Box, "With an Eye to the Future, Friends Fashion Flying Car," *Dallas Morning News,* April 7, 2007, archived, n.p.

BIBLIOGRAPHY

When I began my research, I found only one book devoted to the subject of flying cars: *Les Voitures Volantes: Souvenirs d'un Futur Rêvé,* by Patrick J. Gyger (available now in English as *Flying Cars: The Extraordinary History of Cars Designed for Tomorrow's World*), which features science-fiction predictions in classic illustrations. George W. Green's *Flying Cars, Amphibious Vehicles and Other Dual Mode Transports,* which came to my attention later, yielded insights into late-twentieth-century prototypes and peculiar hybrids, such as the helicopter camper. I found two books devoted to specific flying cars. Jake Shultz's *A Drive in the Clouds: The Story of the Aerocar* offers insight into and pictures of important predecessors and contemporaneous prototypes. To support his own design, Daniel R. Zuck wrote *An Airplane in Every Garage,* providing a fascinating geopolitical rationale for the roadable airplane. Bill Yenne's *The World's Worst Aircraft* offers an informative, if critical, chapter titled "Flying Cars and 'Roadable Airplanes.'"

Much of my research was done by following online images to articles or fragments of articles, both positive and negative, concerning unusual air and automotive hybrids over the last century and into this one. The magazines *Popular Mechanics* and *Popular Science* and the PopSci online archives are vast compendiums of imaginative prototypes. Patrick Cooke's *Forbes FYI* article "Sappy Motoring" included the Airphibian as well as the 1958 Ford nuclear-powered prototype, the Nucleon. A *New Yorker* article offered clarification of the term *Dymaxion.* The magazine *Special Interest Autos* ran a particularly interesting overview called "Cars That Fly: Swing High, Sweet Chariot." Other articles identified as sources of quotations were also a resource for general information and photos.

Choosing particular prototypes to illustrate the progression and pitfalls of pursuing the dream of a flying car meant eliminating certain worthy attempts. I apologize, and I recommend the list of patents and patent drawings in *Roadable Aircraft, From Wheels to Wings* by Palmer Stiles, as well as the Roadable Times website, www.roadabletimes.com. In addition, the website www.fiddlersgreen.net is packed with information about the clever historical models they create.

I found wonderful period photographs and background information that helped me place the inventions in their historical and technological context in heavily illustrated histories, including *The Road to Kitty Hawk* by Valerie Moolman and *The Century* by Peter Jennings and Todd Brewster. *Populuxe: The Look and Life of America in the '50s and '60s, from Tailfins and TV Dinners to Barbie Dolls and Fallout Shelters* by Thomas Hine contains images of modern optimism in design. *The World of Flight* by Ian Graham helped me understand the basic vocabulary of small aircraft.

BOOKS AND ARTICLES

Brown, John. *Flugautos aus aller Welt.* Unpublished manuscript. Königswinter, Germany: HEEL Verlag, 2012.

Bryson, Bill. *The Life and Times of the Thunderbolt Kid: A Memoir.* New York: Broadway Books, 2006.

Fulton, Robert Edison, Jr. *One Man Caravan: Robert Edison Fulton's Round-the-World Tour on a Douglas Motorcycle Between July 1932 and December 1933.* North Conway, N.H.: Whitehorse Press, 1937.

Graham, Ian. *The World of Flight.* Boston: Kingfisher, 2006.

Green, George W. *Flying Cars, Amphibious Vehicles and Other Dual Mode Transports: An Illustrated Worldwide History.* Jefferson, N.C.: McFarland, 2010.

Gyger, Patrick J. *Flying Cars: The Extraordinary History of Cars Designed for Tomorrow's World.* Newbery Park, Calif.: Haynes North America, 2011. Originally published as *Les voitures volantes: souvenirs d'un futur rêvé.* Lausanne, Switzerland: Editions Favre, 2005.

Hine, Thomas. *Populuxe: The Look and Life of America in the '50s and '60s, from Tailfins and TV Dinners to Barbie Dolls and Fallout Shelters.* New York: Alfred A. Knopf, 1987.

Jennings, Peter, and Todd Brewster. *The Century.* New York: Doubleday, 1998.

Lomask, Milton. *Great Lives: Invention and Technology.* New York: Atheneum Books for Young Readers, 1991.

Moolman, Valerie. *The Road to Kitty Hawk.* Alexandria, Va.: Time-Life Books, 1980.

Powell, Dennis E. "Winging It—Down the Road, Through the Clouds the Aerocar Is Still Aloft." *The Seattle Times* (Seattle, WA), July 15, 1990.

Schultz, Jake. *A Drive in the Clouds: The Story of the Aerocar.* New Brighton, Minn.: Flying Books International, 2006.

Stiles, Palmer. *Roadable Aircraft, from Wheels to Wings: A Flying Auto and Roadable Aircraft Patent Search.* Melbourne, Fla.: Custom Creativity, 1994.

Weisberger, Bernard A., general consultant. *The Story of America.* Pleasantville, N.Y.: Reader's Digest Association, 1975.

Yenne, Bill. *The World's Worst Aircraft.* Greenwich, Conn.: Dorset Press, 1990.

Zuck, Daniel R. *An Airplane in Every Garage.* New York: Vantage Press, 1958.

ARCHIVAL VIDEO

Jean Marie LeBris

en.wiki-videos.com/video/Jean-Marie+Le+Bris

Gustave Whitehead

www.youtube.com/watch?v=Ucm80BYUXEE

Trajan Vuia

www.youtube.com/watch?v=umFY3GJxKiQ

Leyat Helica

www.youtube.com/watch?v=VnyKNO958OY

Glenn Curtiss

www.criticalpast.com/2.webloc
www.youtube.com/watch?v=#2278C3
curtiss-jn.purzuit.com/v#22791C
Lillian Boyer performing aerial acrobatics on Curtiss JN-4 while in flight in Chattanooga, Tennessee, 1920.

Ford's Flying Flivver

www.youtube.com/watch?v=#227AD3
Ford is shown inspecting his new flivver plane on his birthday, July 30, 1925.

www.youtube.com/watch?v=J2rAFY-IZas
Brooks landing in Washington, 1928.

Waterman's Whatsit

www.youtube.com/watch?v=#22708B
www.criticalpast.com/2.webloc

Pitcairn's Autogiro

www.criticalpast.com/2.webloc
Autogiro jump-start.

www.youtube.com/watch?v=#22EC7B
Autogiro lands in Washington, D.C.

www.youtube.com/.webloc
Pitcairn Autogiro history.

www.youtube.com/watch?v=#22ED1C
Cierva's Pitcairn PA36 autogyro jump takeoff, late 1930s.
This video contains rare historical footage of German Nazi helicopters in action.

GWINN'S AIRCAR

www.criticalpast.com/2.webloc

FULLER'S DYMAXION CAR

www.youtube.com/watch?v=#227367
Amelia Earhart is in the back seat.

STOUT'S SCARAB

www.youtube.com/watch?v=#227134

HALL'S FLYING AUTOMOBILE

www.youtube.com/watch?v=kAX9oVWhywA

FULTON'S AIRPHIBIAN

www.criticalpast.com/2.webloc

TAYLOR'S AEROCAR

www.youtube.com/watch?v=-60kbxW27kM
Narrated by Molt Taylor.

www.youtube.com/watch?v=WiFjhw_Iq9s&feature=related
Aerocar on "I've Got a Secret."

www.youtube.com/watch?v=#227471
"I've Got a Secret" in Spanish.

www.youtube.com/watch?v=#2275BA
Aerocar 3.

PORTER AND KISSELL

www.youtube.com/watch?v=gcT3muJSi-k

ACKNOWLEDGMENTS

One of the great pleasures of working on this book has been meeting—in person, over the phone, or online—enthusiastic and generous people I would likely never have encountered otherwise.

John Brown, editor of *Roadable Times,* author of *Flugautos aus aller Welt* and webmaster of GustaveWhitehead.com, helped me sort through some historical and engineering information that was beyond my limited experience. His willingness to share his unparalleled scholarship on the subject went a long way toward making the book possible.

Jake Shultz started me in the right direction, thanks to his passion for Molt Taylor's Aerocar and Taylor's remarkable book, *A Drive in the Clouds.*

Patrick J. Gyger, former director of La maison d'ailleurs in Yverdon-les-Bains, Switzerland, offered encouragement and the inspiration of his elegant book *Les Voitures Volantes.*

Thanks also to the following:

Rick Leisenring, curator of the Curtiss Museum in Hammondsport, New York, for making the remarkable Autoplane photographs available, and to Dorothy Cochrane and Dom Pisano for letting me take a peek at their curatorial files at the Smithsonian.

Dan Corneliu Hadîrcă, for the extraordinary archival photos of Vuia's airplane-automobile.

Eileen Jeffress, for encouragement and for sharing her knowledge of Daniel Zuck's Plane-Mobile.

Bruce R. Charnov, PhD, Hofstra University, for generously guiding me through the curious history of the autogyro.

Rawn Fulton, for providing family photos and for filling in some gaps in his father's fascinating story.

Craig Harmon, director of the Lincoln Highway National Museum and Archives, who went out of his way to help by searching and sharing the Pitcairn archives.

The Connecticut Discovery Museum, especially Andy Kosch, who reconstructed Gustave Whitehead's 1901 flying automobile to see if the history books had made a mistake, as did the Historical Research Committee of the Deutsches Flugpioniermuseum Gustav Weisskopf, Leutershausen.

I am indebted to the archivists at the National Aeronautics and Space Museum Archive, the Seattle Museum of Flight, the Detroit Historical Society, the Henry Ford Museum, and the San Diego Air and Space Museum for their patience and expertise. And also to Aerofiles, Johann Visschedijk at 1000 Aircraft Photos, Iowa Memories, the Library of Congress, and the Florida archives for their generosity and curious photos, as well as Critical Past Videos.

I owe Dinah Stevenson much gratitude for her patience in directing me away from the merely amusing factoid to the genuine pleasure of discovering and conveying the twists and turns of the quest to construct from the fantasy a new reality in the form of a real flying car.

PICTURE CREDITS

Aerocar.com: 89

Bernard Hoffman/The LIFE Picture Collection/Getty Images: 68 (top left), 68 (top right), 68 (center)

Bill Crump: 94 (above)

Chicago History Museum: 51

Courtesy of Lockheed Martin: 92 (bottom)

Courtesy of Vernon Porter: 94 (inset)

Courtesy, The Estate of R. Buckminster Fuller: 49 (above), 49 (below), 50

Creative Commons: 80 (Crosley poster)

CriticalPast: 33 (bottom), 42 (left), 42 (below)

Dan I. Hadîrcă: 12, 14 (above), 14 (center)

Daniel R. Zuck Trust: 72, 74

Detroit Historical Society: 52, 53, 54

From the collections of The Henry Ford: 30 (top), 55 (left)

G. H. Curtiss Museum, Hammondsport, NY: 18, 20, 21, 22 (below), 22 (right), 23

Garland Landmark Society, Inc.: Frontis, 58

Hargrave Images (public domain): 14 (inset)

Historical Flight Research Committee Gustave Whitehead: 10

Iowa Department of Transportation: 29

Johan Visschedijk, 1000aircraftphotos.com: 45 (top), 45 (bottom)

The Lincoln Highway National Museum and Archives/Hofstra University/Courtesy of the Pitcairn Aviation Archives and Stephen Pitcairn: 37, 38 (top), 38 (bottom), 39, 40 (left), 40 (below), 43

Moller International, USA: 92 (left)

Museum of Flight (Seattle): 77, 78, 81, 82, 83, 84, 86, 86 (inset), 87, 88

Office nationale de la proprieté industrielle (public domain): 11

PAL-V Europe NV: 90 (upper right)

Photographed by the author: 90 (lower left)

Piasecki Aircraft Corporation: 91 (bottom)

RareNewspapers.com (History's Newsstand): 30 (bottom)

Rawn Fulton: 65, 69

Roadable Times: 12, 15

San Diego Air & Space Museum: 33 (top), 34, 35, 46, 55 (below), 57 (above), 57 (below), 59, 60 (top), 61 (top), 61 (center), 61 (bottom), 63

Smithsonian National Air and Space Museum (Washington): 2, 4, 16, 24, 25, 32, 41, 60 (inset), 67, 73

State Archives of Florida, *Florida Memory:* 79

Stiles, *Roadable Aircraft:* 27

Thomas D. McAvoy/The LIFE Picture
   Collection/Getty Images: 68 (bottom)
Urban Aeronautics Ltd.: 93
Wikimedia Commons (public domain): 1, 3,

19, 47, 80 (Ercoupe poster), 85
www.carplane.com: 91 (top)
www.gustave-whitehead.com, John Brown
   Collection: 5, 6, 7, 9

INDEX

Page numbers in **bold** type refer to photos and illustrations.